# DECEIVING THE ELITE CHURCH

*21ST CENTURY WITCHCRAFT*

**Kathleen Spooner**

# Dedication

Dedicated to nineteen young children and two teachers who lost their lives and the many others in my generation to school shootings. Their lives are noticed.

# Acknowledgments

I want to acknowledge Jesus, my Lord, and Savior. I am so grateful to you. Thank you for your love for me and for all the help you have given me. Holy Ghost, so grateful for you and what you do. I wouldn't have done this without you. I am thankful to my Father for receiving my prayers during this whole thing. You have answered lots. I appreciate and thank you so much. Your will be done.

I want to thank John Ramirez for his past mentorship in my life. I want to thank David E. Taylor for coming to me and speaking over my life during this time. I want to thank Greg Yackley for speaking over my life many times. You will be missed. I want to thank Excel Publishing for working with me during this time. I appreciate David Basely for his patience. I want to thank my daughter, Sydney, for her love.

# Contents

# Introduction

I remember years ago, doing a Bible study on Gideon by Priscilla Shirer. She went in depth on the generational failure of sin and captivity. In the Bible, you read of generations of people falling. The generations usually range from grandparents, parents, and their children ranging from one hundred and younger. The generations can go back beyond grandparents, as well. But the fact of the matter is that there is a problem of sins of iniquity and transgression over years and years of people's lives. The iniquity is an inner moral failure of sexual sins or thinking, talking, and viewing perversity and other things. Iniquity can be using curse words that bring curses on people or profanity and coarse talking. Iniquity can be taking advantage of the poor, fatherless, and widows. Transgression is doing wrong with what belongs to someone else. Transgression can be theft or committing adultery with someone who is married to someone else. Transgression is disobeying the commandments of God.

You have missed the laws of traffic and God's laws in some way. Yes. Speeding is a sin. I get that it is tough, and I constantly ask God to help me with this one. Especially when I went six blocks and saw a forty mile per hour sign I just came to. Then, I realized for six blocks; I missed that I was supposed to be driving twenty-five mph. Sometimes this is an extreme mistake, and sometimes it is a sin. Perhaps it was a block, and you missed it. You just couldn't see the sign. You slowed down. If you don't see it. Slow down. It is probably 25 mph on a block. I don't believe this is a sin if you truly are slowing down to get to 25 mph when you realize you are going fast. Just yesterday, I was driving, and I came to a 45mph sign. I sped up from 40 to get to 45 and sped up too fast. I was trying to come down, but I no sooner started, and I went on, and I am now in a 50mph. I never made it down to forty-five mph. I remember once asking a police officer about the way I was crossing the street when I walked, and the light was on a red-hand stop. The officer told me not to worry about it. The intersection is extremely hard to cross. Sometimes, you have to go when you can. He was telling me about a section of town where the road was going truly short from 35mph to 50mph. He wasn't too concerned about the big gap, so quick to pull people over. I understand there are things that we don't need to worry too much about. I am talking about a constant sin issue of not obeying the laws of traffic. The Bible says, *"Submit yourselves to every ordinance of man for the Lord's sake: Whether it be the king, as supreme or unto governors, as unto them that are sent by him for the punishment of evildoers, and for the praise of them that do well. For so is the will of God, that with the well doing ye may put to silence the ignorance of foolish men: as free, and not using your liberty as a cloke of maliciousness, but as the servants of God. Honour all men. Love the brotherhood. Fear God. Honour the king." 1 Peter 2:13-17*

Someone must step up. Christians have the authority in Christ to step up in the gap and rescue the people out of the hand of the enemy. You know it takes the LORD, hearing and answering prayers, to raise up someone to confront the sins for it to change. In today's age, we call these people that step up as warriors for Christ. These are the people who know the times and seasons. They are wise.

It was a pattern in Judges. It was a pattern in the Old Testament. In the New Testament, John the Baptist prepared the way for the Lord. Then, Lord Jesus began to confront, heal, and deliver his very own people. God raises up deliverance ministers who know how to deliver the people from bondages and diseases, and strongholds. God even raises up mighty Generals. This is done through the Lord Jesus and the power of his Holy Spirit. There are two different powers here. Jesus has Exousia power. His power is an office and authority. We are given to tap into his exousia power. The Holy Spirit has an office and power too. It is not the same as Jesus'. His power is Dunamis. The powers are different and used differently. The saint can tap in and use both, but you must be in standing to use them. A saved person can tap into exousia. A Holy Spirit Baptized person can tap into dunamis. There is another power called Kratos. This is the Father's office and power. You cannot tap into this unless you are under Sonship, and a saint who is just saved must walk 20 years before entering this realm. Some have walked longer than 20 years and are not there. You are required to do certain things to tap into this realm. There is a secret beyond the 20-year requirement. It is a great thing, my brother, David E. Taylor revealed called the 3 a.m. prayer secret.

The Lord wants you to know what he has for you in Christ. The Lord wants you to be delivered as a person, whether you are a Christian or not. Did you know that the Word of God is quick? It brings you to life. In the glory realm of heaven, the light of the Father gets rid of all darkness inside us. The glory realm works on us here on earth too. You get renewed by understanding that the Holy Spirit brings to your attention the meaning of Scripture and changes you to be a giver. This way, you can use it, defeat the devil, and live an abundant life. Did you know that the

Word of God is powerful? It can allow the Holy Spirit to activate your armor, and you know the Word and the Word of Truth has set you free. You can be in the offensive position and see the Holy Spirit use you to heal, deliver, set free, and raise the dead.

Did you know that the Word of God is sharper than any two-edged sword? You can learn what it says by reading it. Then, you speak it out in faith and understanding and defeat the enemy with it. Jesus did this while he was in the temptations of the devil. Did you know that the Word of God pierces even to the dividing asunder of soul and spirit? The soul and spirit of a man determine who the Lords are. There can be great oppression by a demon still in the soul of a believer. The word of the Lord is powerful. Look at Saul's case. He was the Lord's and fell into disobedience. This allowed a demon to come upon Saul. The Bible says, *"And it came to pass, when the evil spirit from God was upon Saul, that David took an harp, and played with his hand: so, Saul was refreshed, and was well, and the evil spirit departed from him."* 1 Samuel 16:23. An evil spirit can afflict the soul to great degrees, but through the playing of God's instrument that he likes, the strings, the evil spirit could not stand before God's chosen anointed king. God talks about the instruments he likes in Exodus, Numbers, and even the Psalms.

*Behold, I will bring it health and cure, and I will cure them, and will reveal unto them the abundance of peace and truth. And I will cause the captivity of Judah and the captivity of Israel to return and will build them, as at the first. And I will cleanse them from all their iniquity, whereby they have sinned against me; and I will pardon all their iniquities, whereby they have sinned, and whereby they have transgressed against me. And it shall be to me a name of joy, a praise, and an honour before all nations of the earth, which shall hear all the good that I do unto them: and they shall fear and tremble for all the goodness and for all the prosperity that I procure unto it. Jeremiah 33:6-9*

# Chapter 1

This work was done at a time when apostasy was great in the United States of America. There are great acts of refusing to follow and obey the Bible and Jesus Christ. Thus, I began this work in the spring of 2022 in the Midwest. The work is addressed to the whole church. I am using illustrations from work here to show the church the things that are done in the eyes of all mankind. Consequently, the church will be able to rid itself of such things. These are abominations and considered iniquities if we involve ourselves in such entanglements of behavior. There is a large famine in the Word of God, the Bible (Actual Scriptures). There are real people who speak for men and women but have never read the Bible from Genesis to Revelation seven times. If you want to give your opinion in this world, tell me you have read it or listened seven times. Have you read it six times? Have you read it five times? Have you read it four times? Have you read it three times? Have you read it two times? Have you read it once? If you have read it or listened once and did not believe, read it again. Then, come and talk to me. Have you met and talked to Jesus Christ in person? Have you had a dream or vision and directly spoken with God or Jesus or the Holy Spirit face to face? My name is

Kathleen Ryan Spooner. You may have read it on the cover. The name Kathleen means pure, clean, transparent, and open. The name Ryan means little king, ruler, kingly. The name Spooner means spoon, chip, or splinter, a tool used for covering with wooden roof shingles. Therefore, if I go by my name to glorify my life to God the Father, Son, and Holy Spirit, it is to be cleaned by Jesus Christ and transparent, to rule with faith, justice, love, and mercy, and to use the skill of occupation to repair and beautifully cover those in my path. Yes, I pray for you constantly. I pray for all people in the world, saved and unsaved, every day. I love you very deeply and want you to have the Lord change your life. This is his work to change you to be like Christ.

I want to express that before you read this book, the first thing to note is love. Without love, we are nothing. I don't want people to feel condemned. I have sinned a lot in my life. In fact, I have sinned a lot as a Christian. There is no one time you get saved, and don't sin anymore. It is a lie. We do become holy, but the fact that no one sins after they come into Christianity is a lie. In fact, Christians commit huge sins. If you left the church because you thought the Christians were judgmental of you or acted as though your sins were too bad for them. This is wrong. There is no one person on this earth who hasn't committed sin. Perhaps, an infant, but as soon as a child starts to grow, they sin. The Christian gets saved and is supposed to turn from sins. But they need help from God to stop their sins. I know I need help. The difference is that a Christian has the Lord, Holy Spirit, and his Baptism to help them from sinning. He is the one who helps you overcome, and the Father can remove temptations and make a way of escape. You stop because the Holy Spirit works on your mind, attitude, and emotions. He is the one who gives you the power to turn away from things that hurt you. I know people stop going to church because they believe the people in the church are wrong. However, don't be deceived; this is a tool of the devil to get you out of the church community and on your own thoughts. This is how he gets into your home, mind, and body. He steals your relationships, community, and belonging to the church. You can be a Christian that doesn't go to church, but I wouldn't advise it. It is a sin unless you are homebound and cannot in no way leave your home to go there. You can be shut away for seasons. The purpose of the shut away is a time of deep prayer and the presence of God. If you felt unloved by the church people at a building you attended, don't listen to the devil. These same people are the reason you got saved, to begin with. The Lord answered their prayers. If you feel that the people at church didn't show you love. Then, you are deceived. The Lord answered their prayers to work in your life to get you back to him. If you felt that they were not as loving to you as God is. Perhaps, but God teaches truth too. The same truth he teaches from the Bible is the truth you hear from the pulpit. If not, then the person teaching it is not teaching correctly. Jesus teaches that you are to go to a church that teaches the Baptism of the Holy Spirit, Righteousness, Holiness, and about Hell. Jesus does not want you to stay if they are not teaching this way. You must leave and find a church teaching these things right away. If you feel they were not loving because they did spiritual warfare prayers, and you were the recipient of some sort. God has tough love too. You were wandering and experiencing tough love from worldly hurts because God allowed it. It is the way he uses life's situations to help you see he is the only way. I have heard too many people say the church building I will not attend because the people in it are not loving. These same people have prayed, and God answered their prayers to help you while you were in the world. The reason you didn't understand this is that you have these strongholds in your mind that the enemy built, so you couldn't discern love in the church. In fact, the Christian who continues in sins and iniquity can lose their salvation and go to hell. The Bible says it, not me. *"The righteousness of the righteous shall not deliver him in the day of his transgression. When I say to the righteous, that he shall surely live; if he trusts to his own righteousness, and commit iniquity, all his righteousness shall not be remembered; but for the iniquity that he committed, he shall die for it. When the righteous turneth from his righteousness, and committeth iniquity, he shall even die thereby"* Ezekiel 33:12,13,18. This means that you better know the Bible. We are all to be held accountable to the words written therein. You can get saved and follow the Lord. But you must ensure you stay saved under the Lord. There is not once saved always saved in the Bible. Jesus saves you, but you are to make sure you follow him. There is much to learn from the Bible. The way you learn is by reading it and being taught by your teachers and leaders in the church. You learn by the Holy Spirit teaching you directly too. You can learn by Jesus teaching you. You can learn from the Father teaching you. There are different examples in the Bible of direct teaching from all three persons of the Godhead. It is even in the New Testament.

When I was about 20 years old, I was not yet married but had dated a man since fifteen. His mother told me that I was her Ruth, and she was my Naomi. She said we would always be together. We were in a hotel room. We had traveled to Ohio. We were at an Amway Convention. I reminded her years later of this conversation. She didn't remember it. But I always remembered it. There were years I wandered away from the truth. But I came back. This cannot be taken from me. She is a Christian, and I am a follower of Jesus Christ too. I will remember this beautiful thing she spoke over my life. It was a prophecy. Right after, I began much testing. Now, when something like this gets spoken over you, it is up to you to ensure that you follow it all the way home. I didn't always follow it out. But my God ensured that I had praying people over my life to get me back. I remember in 2016, I was at a public high school. There were a few churches there to give food and drinks to the people at the Homecoming football game. This was something that my church did every year. Another church was next to us, serving nachos while we served snacks and water. The church next to us happened to be the church my daughter grew up in and my ex mother and father-in-law still go to. Though I haven't been with their son since 2010, they are still a mother and father to me. I introduced myself to the woman next to me that was serving nachos with her husband and family. She said, 'Wow! We prayed for you for a long time.' Therefore, don't misunderstand the opportunities the

Lord gives you to repent. The prayers of your mother and father and the righteous avails.

## Times and Seasons

The American Church is behind in understanding times and seasons. There is a battle in the heavens, and a big portion of the church is not fighting it. There needs to be more in the church in line with the Word of God. Jesus requires praying people. Jesus requires deliverance ministers. If you want to overcome these things in the church, you must first take down the demons that are in you. You must come to Christ and receive the forgiveness of your sins and ask him to come into your life and be your LORD. When you allow God to come into your life through Christ, you have now crossed over from death to life. God is the God of the living, not the dead. There are religions out there, like Hinduism, that teach you to reincarnate. This is wrong. You do not reincarnate. You are brought to life in your spirit man, once you die if you have accepted Christ and become his child. You live like an angel of God. You do not marry anymore, but you minister to God. The Bible says, *"And Jesus answering…Do ye not, therefore, err, because ye know not the scriptures, neither the power of God? For when they shall rise from the dead, they neither marry nor are given in marriage; but are as the angels which are in heaven. And as touching the dead, that they rise: have ye not read in the book of Moses, how in the bush God spake unto him, saying, I am the God of Abraham, and the God of Isaac, and the God of Jacob? He is not the God of the dead, but the God of the living: ye, therefore, do greatly err."* Mark 12:24-27.

There is the fact that, as a Christian, you suffer a lot of demonic things. If you have become a Christian, the demons can still have access to your life and appear as though they have possession of you. But in truth, they should not have possession anymore. The Bible says, *"Then I will sprinkle clean water upon you, and ye shall be clean: from all your filthiness, and from all your idols, will I cleanse you. A new heart also will I give you, and a new spirit will I put within you: and I will take away the stony heart out of your flesh, and I will give you a heart of flesh. And I will put my Spirit within you, and cause you to walk in my statutes, and ye shall keep my judgments and do them. Jesus answered...If a man love me, he will keep my words: and my Father will love him, and we will come unto him, and make our abode with him."* *Ezekiel 36:25-27; John 14:23*

When you are saved and Baptized with the Holy Ghost, you now have the Spirit of God living in you and moving you to follow God the Father's commands. The words of Jesus are the Father's words. God is three persons, but one God. If you want all three, you come in by accepting Jesus' sacrifice on the cross for your sins, His burial, and resurrection on the third day. He did what you couldn't. He didn't sin. His blood was pure, and he had no sin. Therefore, Jesus had the right to defeat Satan and the legal rights he had over mankind. But we, as Christians, give our legal rights to the enemy. Though we are saved, we give Satan and demons access to our lives by giving the devil legal rights through accepting his lies. This leads us into bondage and puts up strongholds in our minds, and makes our bodies go downhill through infirmity. The devil and demons have no legal rights, but they can steal ours. Some people have oppression from the outside of a demon riding upon them. Some can even have possession of a demon in their soul or body. For example, when someone prays, they could manifest a demonic power. They can move their hands, and their voices can manifest a demon too. If you are saved and Spirit Baptized, you have the Spirit of God living in you. He came into your spirit. You are now freed from demons living in your spirit. You may think I am out of my mind with this one. But it is a reality. Jezebel has steps of attacking Christians. One of those steps is attacking the anointed. Another is attacking the anointing. I want to expound on this, but I will not in this book. The unsaved person has demons that possess their spirit man. The demons can be sent out of their spirit man, but it is not wise. If you do deliverance by kicking out Satan or demons on a person who is unsaved, the person will end up worse. The Bible says, *"When the unclean spirit is gone out of a man, he walketh through dry places, seeking rest, and findeth none. Then, he saith I will return into my house from whence I came out; and when he comes, he findeth it empty, swept, and garnished. Then goeth he, and taketh with himself seven other spirits more wicked than himself, and they enter in and dwell there: and the last state of that man is worse than the first. Even so, shall it be also unto this wicked generation?"* Matthew 12:43-45. For example, a person gets saved and delivered, then quickly falls away and truly is not saved. This way, the demons can come back seven times stronger. The other way is you cast out demons from an unsaved person who has asked you to pray for them and cast them out. But the person went away and was fine for a bit, but the demons came back to that house (man's spirit) and brought with them seven others.

The demons come back seven times stronger and hurt the person more. I have found that happened in my life. I was saved young. I started going to church at eleven. I was baptized and water baptized at 12. I was saved. I walked with my feet in the world. Then, at 17, I got re-water baptized and went to another church. I continued in the world, and eventually, the world overtook me. When I was around twenty-three, I decided to choose a man over God, and it went bad after that. This was the same man I had been with since I was fifteen. My pastor came into my home and told me that it was not right to be living with the father of my child as married people should live. When my boyfriend got home (who later became my husband), I told him what the pastor said and thought he would want to marry me, finally. He told me to choose God or him. I made the wrong choice, and a lot of demonic things came in after that. I had never seen the darkness in my life as it was after that day. I was not a partying woman. I went to church and worked and raised a child. But that decision cost me my livelihood and stole from me for years.

# Chapter 2 - Kingdom Child

The saved person can manifest by the enemy oppressing their soul and body from the outside and the inside. They live around you and follow you. They implant themselves in your thoughts and mind. They live in your home because you need deliverance from things of your life that you have given Satan legal rights and access to. The enemy can oppress the body of a Christian. I know this sounds unbiblical, but your soul and body are not your spirit man. A demon can occupy you by oppressing you. If this is so, then you need deliverance. The person that is a Christian, in this case, may have an infirmity in the body that never leaves. Another is a person that is a Christian who has dabbled in witchcraft. You wear charm necklaces, read horoscopes, visit psychics, and listen to voices that you believe are the Holy Spirit but are familiar spirits. These kind goeth out by prayer and fasting. You will still need a deliverance minister or another Christian that understands these things to help you. You will need to renounce things in your life that the enemy has had a stronghold and has held you in bondage with. You could have a child that was born with autism or down syndrome. These are generational curses. You could, in this case, be dealing with demons' traveling the bloodline. Even the doctors ask you what your father and mother's health and social life were like. Did they drink, smoke, have cancer, and so forth? This is a generational curse line of demons. These demons could have access to the Christians too. There are a handful of things a Christian might need deliverance from. Demons that entered at some point in your life through something you did or generational demons that travel. The Christian that gets saved does get deliverance from things. You will know you have a change of mind about things. But you will also recognize there are things with which you are still struggling. The Christian that has deliverance in areas of their life must renew and build areas to not ever let the enemy get the upper hand in those areas again. If you were a sexually immoral person or have been delivered from any sin, you need to understand that you must read the Bible and study it. You need to be in a community, and yes, this means going to church. You must renew your mind and get strong in the LORD, to not let the enemy be able to bring another person into your life to take you down. You must know that you will be tempted, but if you do not know what the LORD says about you and know that you know what he says, you will be swayed when you are on the way in some sort. You might be working and having a great day in the Lord. He could be using you to witness multiple times that day while you are working. You are even seeming to be making money. But you notice attacks at the end of the day on your way home. You drive by a store, and a thought comes into your mind. The thought says I had a long day and could use a drink. The funny feeling you get in your mind shows you that maybe a drink might be nice because it was quite a day. It is Friday. Then, another thought comes into your mind that says I could use a pizza and you give in to the thought because the feeling with it is the same feeling of a great desire. You don't recognize it was the enemy. Demons tempt you. You are set up to go into that store because there are strongholds in your mind and that neighborhood, for a fact, too, that allowed you to be tempted right there at that intersection. If the temptation was someone asking you to have lunch with them from a man or woman, but you have a check. You know the enemy will use the same type of man or woman you came out of a hard and bad relationship with to bring you down. The person might have a different name and skin color or ethnicity, but it is the same person in a different outfit. I mean that person will bring the same sins into your life of strongholds that you came out of with another person. You let the enemy bring you into the bar to drink or to say yes to someone that hits on you anywhere at any time.

The Word of God will be how you get strengthened. You will need to read it constantly and build your relationship with the Lord. You will need to hear your pastor preach to get the junk off too. This is how I have been strengthened. I get up and sing to Lord. I magnify his Name. I magnify him. I read the Bible and pray. I do this every day. I usually end the day by spending time with him too. You cannot get enough of the Lord. Can you do this? Yes. What about the areas I am struggling with, Kathleen? I do these things. You may need to do more.  Are you in community with believers? Are you in unity in Christ? Do you go to church? Do you serve?  Do you know Bible verses? Do you witness? Are you in need of deliverance? Do you have strongholds in your mind? Do you have racism? Are you judgmental? Do you preach Jesus? Do you invite people to church? Do you bring down the church through your words? Do you build up the pastors? Do you pray for them constantly? Do you see their weaknesses? Pray. Do you pray for the people in the church the way you pray for yourself? Do you have sickness and disease, and it has made you numb, and you complain? Do you complain often?

Satan and his depths can play you through a living person (human being). These human beings can have a contract with a demon to put oppression on you to kill, steal and destroy your life. This is how it works:

You have a neighbor that hates you. They go to the devil's playground and ask a Satanist to stop you from succeeding. They pay the Satanists money. The Satanist then gets a contract with a bad angel to take your finances away, your relationships away, your family apart, and your livelihood away, so you no longer thrive. Let's look at it from the Bible. The Bible says, *"Balaam, the son of Bosor, who loved the wages of unrighteousness. And Israel abode in Shittim, and the people began to commit whoredom with the daughters of Moab. And they called the people unto the sacrifices of their gods: and the people did eat and bowed down to their gods. And Israel joined himself unto Baal-Peor: and the anger of the LORD was kindled against Israel. But I have a few things against thee because thou hast there them that hold the doctrine of Balaam, who taught Balac to cast a stumbling block before the children of Israel, to eat things sacrificed unto idols, and to commit fornication. 2 Peter 2:15; Numbers 25:1-3; Revelation 2:14.* Therefore, the person of the kingdom of Satan accepts wages from a person to put demons on you to bring you down. They make a contract with a spirit. The kingdom of darkness now brings sexual immorality and falsehood to lead you to commit idolatry against your God. There is a lot more on this subject that I will be expounding on in this book.

A demon can be in the home and even oppress the soul or the body of a believer. As said, when you are saved, the spirit is saved. The soul and body of a believer can still be dealing with demons in your life that have been there for your whole life. The demon may have entered through a generational curse. It can be there for the reason that you allow it to be. I went for prayer for years in the church and went and asked for private prayer. I went to so many pastors and leaders, and I was not any better than before. After years of trying to be free, I finally understood that the church is not prepared to cast out demons. I had little to no understanding of how to pray against Satanic and spiritual warfare. I had no understanding that my family has been under an curse for a lot of years. If you give counsel that the person just needs to read their Bible and know the Word and speak it and go to church, this isn't all believers need. Sometimes, we need another's helping to be delivered. I read my Bible every day, first thing in the morning and usually before I go to bed. I have read it all every year for years now. I read the whole thing every year. I know many verses. I pray. I go to church. I tithe. People need deliverance and need to know how to be delivered. There was one woman who I called the prayer tower for prayer more than once. Why have a 24-hour prayer tower and give bad counsel? I asked for prayer about the same thing. She said, 'I will pray no more. You go and read your Bible, and don't call here no more.' What? At least Kenneth Copeland's Ministry is nice. They told me if I needed to call several times a day to call. Look, it's not always easiest to tell the people close to you what you are going through. Now, I am with the Kingdom of God Global Church. I couldn't be more grateful for Apostle Taylor as a mentor.

# Chapter 3 - My Story

This is a whole retreat center that teaches witchcraft. They are known for all religions, but they teach witchcraft and one mixed religion.

I have a hard time telling this story, but it needs to be told. I meet Satanists and even meaningful Christians that have been in the same situation I have been in or are there now. When I say Satanists, I am talking about witches, wizards, warlocks, sorcerers, root workers, magicians, high priests, witch doctors, etc. When I talk about the church of Satan, you will find them in your community called a Ba'hai school, Metaphysical church, New Age, Spiritual Light, Spiritualist Church, etc. The reason has a lot to do with generational curses. It is something that is passed from a parent on to you. But you didn't get into the demonic manifestations of it heavy until the devil (one depth of Satan) had you right where he wanted you and then struck. The devil struck because he didn't want to lose you, or he had an opportune time because you took the bait he set you up with.

How could the devil set you up and strike? A Christian celebrates Halloween or has a family that has celebrated it through the generations. A Christian has had a witch in their family bloodline. Perhaps, you were the reason. You opened a door in your life to Satan by going to a witch. My mother was into witchcraft. She read tarot cards; I know she did the Ouija board too. She put the witchcraft away. I remember her strongly urging me never to play the Ouija board. The demon killed one of her friends she played it with the night the three of them played it last. The demon announced to the man they were playing it with that he would die that night, and he did. The man that died had a closed casket. My mother said she opened it, and his face looked like Frankenstein. He was shot in the head.

I know my neighbors were into witchcraft heavily. I am not sure if this is how she got into it because she broke the relationship with them. However, she didn't prevent us from playing with the kids in their families. I am sure this wasn't always the best idea, but I was a kid. I didn't understand in my mind about evil spirits. These spirits had nothing on me. I didn't believe they existed. I was fearless. My mother died of a heart infirmity when I was fifteen. She died too young for me. I don't remember her being happy much. Yes, she laughed and had a love for others. But she seemed to have an inner depression if you ask me. She had demons that she needed to be free from. We were not churchgoers. We went on Easter when I was eleven and younger. We were just like the other secular American families that believed we were Christians but had no evidence of it. If you go to church and read your Bible, you will learn what a Christian really is.

Anyhow, my mother had fits of rage (negative Samson spirit), control (Jezebel spirit), and a hold on her that wasn't broken. Not that she did the same things, but that she still needed deliverance. My mother was very good to us children. She was a loving mother and always took care of us. I am only trying to highlight my home life and the demons that entered generationally. I know we hear of lust spirits. Yes, a person can have lust, but there is a root that needs to be dealt with for the inward and outward manifestations to go. Do you remember Lamech, that had two wives? Do you remember King Solomon, Rehoboam, and several down the line? You will hear it when someone points out how good-looking movie stars and musicians are. You will hear it when you still hear the people around you say, Man, look how good-looking that person is who is a leader or in the crowd. That person could be married or even a person of crude talking and behavior. But someone will still point out how they look and that they find them very attractive and would marry them. We watched secular movies and television. We watched Porky's, Elvira, and The Twilight Zone. We watched every show that seemed to be on television at night and soap operas back in the day.

My father was a good dad. He was always there for us too. He liked to take me with him everywhere, even to work on the weekend jobs. His weekday job was too hard for me to go to, but he did take me to school and pick me up. We went on walks and talked and played ball together at the baseball diamond. He was a good dad and very involved in my school life. My mother controlled the house, though. He was a man who had demons attached to him too. He would tell me you may not marry an African American man because there would be too many problems (racist spirit). He would talk about others' business (gossip spirit). He would say the Bible was written by man and not by God (falsehood spirit). He was passive (Ahab spirit). I only tell you these things so you understand the things you can pick up in your life from home. There are real demons, and they can transfer from person to person. These are demons that know more than you about this earth. I am not putting my parents down. I desire to have them again. I want to be a family. It is extremely hard to walk this earth without your parents. I am explaining how demons get access to us and what happens after that. Every person on this earth has a demon that follows them around all the time. The Lord put angelic beings that fell from heaven here to test us. Lucifer was our brother, but he didn't like us from the beginning. Satan, fallen angels and demons hate human beings. There are a lot of things to learn about them and that you should know. The demons work under Satan, Principalities, Rulers (King demons), and Beelzebub (Prince of Hell, not Satan). I want to honor my parents, who were loving. If they were still here, I would have learned a lot and learned how to fight in prayer better. I am fighting for my family now. I remember the last time I saw my dad; I had learned some spiritual warfare. He couldn't even raise his head to look at me. I had not seen him in five and half years. It was spiritual. I would talk to him, and he wouldn't raise his head. I was alone with him and prayed several spiritual warfare prayers. Guess what? His head raised, and he could look at me. Those spirits had to leave with the power of Christ's blood. I want every person to know that these demons are evil, and they will destroy your family if allowed to. Falsehood and Gossip are spirits. Ahab, Delilah, and Samson are spirits that took on negative forms of past human beings. The spirit of racism is demonic. My mother had an understanding. But the spirits still had a stronghold, and that stronghold needed to break. My mother always told us, children, to stay together and, when she died to never let anything separate us. Why? She understood that witchcraft was a tool of the devil. "In my past life as a devil worshipper, I was taught and trained to have no mercy in attacking the family through witchcraft to break their unity and separate them from one another, especially if they were married."[2]

I didn't take her advice and heed it in life but allowed devils to wreak havoc upon my family. I didn't understand that the enemy came in and allowed my family to be separated through thoughts, patterns, and cycles. The familiarity needs to be broken. The devil uses patterns of cycles of repeat to dismantle the family and get them to hate one another. Pride comes in, and words bring hurt. I don't hate anyone in my family. But my own words have hurt. I fell big with pride. This is a tool of the devil. I remember when my mom died, pride started to take hold of my life. I fell hard in life to understand this. Pride is a spirit. God used for good what Satan meant for evil in my life. I was abused, beaten, and tortured in my life for a season. God used this to break a controlling and prideful spirit in me.

In my early years, my family was very secular. We did things most secular families did that are family oriented. We did things together. But our wants and desires resembled the life of unbelievers. I see a lot of Christian families that lived as we did, and we didn't go to church every Sunday like them. We didn't get the Bible read to us in the house. I recall my mother reading the Bible one time from cover to cover, but she read the Mormon Book that way too. Another neighbor went to that church. Perhaps, this is why she was reading it. She was searching for help with her inner troubles. She was searching for the truth. Maybe she was reading it to minister the right truth to them. We never went to a Mormon church.

We attended church on Easter before I was eleven that taught about the Triune God. She thought Jesus was the answer, but she had no root. Root, this is the problem with a lot of people. I see people get saved, but they have no roots. They claim they are Christians because they had decided one time in their life to follow Christ and were water baptized. But the Bible is clear when you have no root. You last for a short time, and then you fall away. You hear these people tell you they are Christians. They celebrate Easter and Christmas. They don't go to church. They have a meal in their home and open presents and call themselves Christians, who are good people and will go to heaven when they die. They know not the Scriptures and that this is not a Christian at all. They have been deceived by Satan and his workers of evil. Their home is hell when they die unless they get saved on their deathbed. I was a person like this. I believed I would go to heaven and was good. I had accepted Jesus and been saved. But I fell away. I didn't get it.

# Root

Root means you have a prayer life. It doesn't mean you pray every night. I lay myself down to sleep, and I pray for my family and name them. It means you have a prayer life. You know how to use your prayer life and are active in it all day and night and are even a watchful Christian and know the times and seasons. They have no root in their giving. Most people here in this group, calling themselves Christians, will tell you that I don't need to go to church to be a Christian. Did you read the Bible? The Bible makes this clear. You know, I even have Christians telling me that I don't need to go to a church building to be a Christian. These Christians, I have found, have been hit with a delusional spirit. This spirit has accompanied their life. They were hit by the leader Ahab, one year. That Ahab brought into their life through ground demons who operate under Ahab's authority to put laziness and to slumber, and passivity. They got hit with passivity. They are passive people. I see these Christians, who I have been, by the way, get pulled away by the teachings of the wind. These wind teachings tell them other things that seem good to the ears. The Good to the Ear's teachings have some Christian truths mixed in them.

When you get into places of witchcraft, there are familiar spirits coming to talk to you. They come into the home of the Christian and live there. Then, the Christian starts reading the Bible and believes the Holy Spirit is speaking to them, and you have the spirit appearing as an angel of light talking to them. Please understand that when God kicked his high angel, Lucifer, out of heaven that there were complexities of his being created to deceive mankind. He hated Adam, and he would not bow to Adam as God asked when he created him. Thus, his pride got the best of him, and he asked God to allow him to name the animals instead of Adam. God said okay and allowed Lucifer to have an opportunity to name the animals. He was not able. Then, Adam had a chance. Adam was given in his being when created to be a prophet. He understood the names just because God gave him that in his being at creation. Adam named them. Lucifer started down a very bad path after this that kept getting worse. These truths are found in ancient Jewish scripts. Lucifer then started on his depths. His highest complexity is the fallen one. He creates evil daily. The angel of light is one complexity. Demons know all about you. They know your likes, dislikes, character, and so on. They tell you things, and you can't discern it is not the Holy Spirit because you think I was baptized with the Holy Spirit. I hear the Holy

Spirit. You may have been baptized, but you can be tricked if you have allowed something else to enter your home. This tricking spirit has been telling you things that seem good. You think that because it is good, it is coming from the Holy Spirit. You think because you don't have anything bad coming from this thought that, it is God. No. No. No. They mimic God. They copy. They treat you well and act good but are, in fact, a demon. If you find this out or at some point catch up, it might be a demon. The demon's true self will show up, and you will be aware of how they really act when you have learned. God will show you the truth about this situation, especially if you enter weeks of fasting for someone else. God will show you things about yourself that are not right. Then, the demon will show you their true self. These spirits could have entered when you did a seance and believed you met with your mother or father. They can come and pretend to be your mother talking to you. They can manifest her character completely because they knew her. You may have brought them home by having your tarot cards read too.

The root of giving is in the Bible, both in the Old and New Testaments. Jesus said to give your tithe. *"Woe unto you scribes and Pharisees, hypocrites! For ye pay tithe of mint and anise and cummin and have omitted the weightier matters of law, judgment, mercy, and faith: these ought to have done, and not to leave the other undone"* Matthew 23:23. If you believe this only refers to oils in your giving. This is not accurate either. Tithing and finances are God's use of helping the church to spread the Kingdom Gospel of Jesus Christ to the ends of the world. If this isn't important to you, then the lives of people's eternal homes aren't probably either. People must be sent, and often the use of finances is the whole reason the community is provided for when they cannot afford food, water, electricity, and much more. It is the church that is there to pray,

and the reason finances are used. If the finances come from someone outside the church. The Lord used you as an answer to someone's prayer he heard. It also says not to come before him during the three annual feasts empty-handed. Celebrating feasts is talked about in the New Testament too. Dig it out. I did. These are offerings. Offerings are referred to as the amount after you have paid your tithe. These are to support ministries. The Bible is clear about giving in Malachi 3. Also, God will not be able to use any child effectively in their life if they are not a person of faith in this area. I have heard that there is a special place in hell for the people who were not faithful in paying tithes. I have not seen the pit, but I heard Apostle David Taylor tell of a time when God took him to hell, and he saw Christians in a pit. Jesus told him this pit was for not being faithful to their tithe. Tithes are paid. This is not your offering. The Bible says we pay our tithes. They are the required ten percent before we give. They are out of our gross paycheck. If you just get the net, as soon as it hits your account, tithe off of the gross. God says the first ten percent belongs to him. Don't worry about taxes. You pay for those too. Jesus said to give to God what belongs to him and to Caesar (tax man) what belongs to him. We have churches that don't even stick to this teaching. They explain that it is not for the people of today and give you Scriptures that line up with their teaching. I would not listen to them. In the New Testament, Jesus talked a lot about finances. Read the Bible for yourself. Did you know that Shem lived until he was six hundred years old, and his father, Noah, lived for 950 years? Abraham was born in Noah's latter years, and Shem was around 399 years old when Abraham was born. Check it out; it is recorded in Genesis. Also, the book of Jasher goes into the account of the ages of these men. Melchizedek is said to have no mother or father, beginning and end in Hebrews 7. In the Bible, you hear of an account of Melchizedek, where Abraham gave him a tenth. Noah and Seth took Abraham in when he was running from Nimrod, who tried to kill him. Why would

Abraham have known to give him a tenth? Noah and Seth raised Abraham up in the ways of the LORD.

The root of their thought life is not right either. They would rather believe demons' thoughts and that the thoughts in their mind are their own all the time. It is not so. Satan and demons often afflict the soul, mind part and thoughts with a setup thought to get you to commit sin. It is like you are okay and good, but you believe the demons' thoughts and follow their course of thinking. Recall they appear as angels of light in your thoughts and tell you good things. They do this for a reason. It is to dupe you into their setups. They will be able to bring you down by doing this. We, as people, are called to be a part of God's family. We are called to be merciful to others. I have fallen in this area for sure. I am merciful. But have fallen. Any time we put someone up on our Facebook or social media and say something against them to defame them, this is unmerciful. When we don't stop this behavior, we end up in hell for it. This includes Christians who don't repent from this sin.

I didn't get lustful thoughts, but I had no root in giving gratitude to God. I thought when I heard them that if others thought this strongly about someone to love on television, I must have those thoughts too. I didn't, but I tried hard to find them. I thought, "Okay, I like Mr. Belvedere. There is a kid on that show my age. I'll pick him." I didn't have lust, but I tried to fabricate it. I cut his picture out of a magazine. My parents bought me Teen Magazine, Tiger Beat, Seventeen, and Cosmopolitan, and on one occasion, because I asked for it, a rolled-up Astrology/Horoscope thing at the Supermarket. This is wrong! If you are a parent buying these, you are probably in the world. I get it. You are most likely not a Christian. These things teach lust, sex, witchcraft, and many other worldly things. I put Brice Beckham's picture in a five-sevenths frame and said, I guess I'll love him. You know demons are real; they hear. This was an opportunity for them to lead me into lustful thoughts. I tried to pick a New Kid's on the Block man, too, like my sisters. Satan's demons took me for a mile with the inch I gave. I heard nasty rap music that talks about the steps you give a man in sex through a pornographic mind. I memorized these words as a kid too. This is a demonic setup to get me to lust. I am sure that my life was more out of control than my sisters. They have excelled and are helping their families. I am so grateful for them. I love them. I want to point out how Satan and demons took my life for a loop and are captivating the minds of the world and his church.

# Chapter 4 - What Do We Need?

The church is not fighting the battle that needs to be fought. My former mentor, John Ramirez, told us that a strong church needs to have a deliverance minister and some people who know how to do spiritual warfare as an intercessor. The church is used to having regular intercessors. These are good, but there needs to be spiritual warfare ones too. The reason is this. The church is sick. Why? There aren't enough deliverance ministers and true Apostles helping people. There aren't enough spiritual warfare intercessors. I believe that confusion is in the church when it comes to someone doing warfare in the heavens over the moon and stars. There is confusion when it comes to a Christian looking at someone's past and what their life is today. You can be a spiritual warfare watcher and prayer warrior and not be into astrology. Further, there is so much witchcraft that has been in the lives of the Christian families that they look at spiritual warfare against the church of Satan in a light that the person who is a Christian is into things of Satan when they try to explain how to defeat it. Defeating it by using terms that are scary to Christians is needed, but you will find people shying away from hearing you when their life is not hearing you because the enemy has a stronghold on them in that area, and he doesn't want them to be free. I will explain it to you further in the book.

We see that many churches believe that the Christians, once saved, have the Holy Spirit and no longer can have demons. Well, the demons are making a laugh at the Christians by running rampant in their homes through the oppression that is hidden from the mind of the believer. You are oppressed by demons because you don't know you have them in your home and lodging themselves in the soulish realm in your thoughts and mind. Additionally, they lodge in your body realm by oppressing you from the outside with sickness and disease. You may have allowed them to do this through your words. You came into agreement with their words, and now they have legal rights. Can a Christian have demons inside their soul or body? Yes.

If this wasn't so, then why did Jesus cast out so many demons in the Bible with his own people? They can be cast out whether they are in or outside the person oppressing them. Do you remember the woman that was bound for 18 years? He called her a daughter of Abraham. He referred to others who talked bad to him about his miracles that were

Jews and went to the synagogue (church) as children of the devil (John 8:44). The key point is that you can sit in church, believe in Jesus, and come to him for your healing and deliverance and salvation, or you can sit there and not believe in him. If you do the latter, you will ultimately not be his child, and you will be called by Him a child of the devil.

*"And he was teaching in one of the synagogues on the Sabbath. And behold, there was a woman who had a spirit of infirmity eighteen years, and was bowed together, and could in no wise lift up herself. And when Jesus saw her, he called her to him and said to her, woman, thou art loosed from thine infirmity. And he laid his hands on her: and immediately she was made straight, and glorified God. And the ruler of the synagogue answered with indignation, because that Jesus had healed on the Sabbath day, and unto the people, there are six days in which men ought to work: in them therefore come and be healed, and not on the Sabbath day. The Lord then answered him and said, thou hypocrite, doth not each one of you on the Sabbath loose his ox or his ass from the stall and lead him away to watering? And ought not this woman, being a daughter of Abraham, whom Satan hath bound, lo, these eighteen years, be loosed from this bond on the Sabbath day? And when he had said*

*these things, all his adversaries were ashamed: and all the people rejoiced for all the glorious things that were done by him." Luke 13:11-17*

Remember that you cannot have demons in you unless you welcome them in as a Christian. Christians that have not been Baptized with the Holy Spirit could have a lodging demon in their body. You may have allowed them in. Generational demons are factors, too, and there are real scrolls and banners against your children and you. There is also the fact that a Christian cannot be cursed. If you believe the witches are putting curses on you, similar to Balaam. You cannot have them put curses on you. You are blessed according to the Word of the Lord. The Bible says the only way you can receive a curse is if you have disobeyed God. If you disobey God, you can get cursed. The Bible says that Balaam could not curse the people of Israel. So, guess what? He put a stumbling block before them. Then, the Israelites were deceived and allowed curses to come. If you fall into disobedience and sinfulness, you open yourself up to curses. So, the witches and wizards tear down and fragment Christians through demons. Satan himself knows this, and he allows them to put demonic-filled people in the way of Christians to get them to sin and disobey God. Now, please understand that eating food sacrificed to idols and sinning sexually is not the only way to disobey God. There are other ways of disobedience. Please read the Bible. You can sin in more than one way through disobedience.

There are parts of the church that don't believe in the gifts of the Spirit being active and that praying in tongues is needed. In the Bible, we read that prayer is part of the armor in Ephesians 6. It tells us that we are to pray in the Holy Spirit. If this gift were not intended for all Christians, why would it be part of our armor? Now there are Christians and pastors that do pray in the Spirit and still don't have spiritual warfare intercessors or deliverance ministers in the church. This is wrong. If you were taught that praying in tongues is wrong, you might be understanding only part. There is a tongue that is for a message in the congregation that is heard and needs an interpreter. This is different than the private tongue you use when you are at home or alone. This tongue is needed, but this tongue can be used in a group of spiritual warfare intercessory groups too. This group knows that there are spiritual warfare tongues the Spirit will use to defeat the enemy of our soul. You may bubble over at church, too, at the altar, or in a pew.

Praying in the Spirit is a gift. It is not the Baptism in the Spirit. The Baptism of the Spirit is when you want more from God. Even Paul asked believers who said they had only the Baptism of John if they had received the Holy Spirit. These believers had received Christ but had not the Holy Spirit. You need this baptism just like the saving baptism and water baptism. I heard a message some time back from Pastor Robert Morris. He taught the baptisms. There are three baptisms. You receive them just like the Jews did when they crossed the Red Sea. They are there as the pattern in the Old Testament of what the LORD would do in the New Testament. Jesus saved you, washed you, and the Holy Spirit came on you with power.

The Holy Spirit is bubbling over in the Father of love. Jesus came out of the Father from Ancient Times. He came out, and so did the Holy Spirit. They are God. We have not three but One God. Father is over the Lord Jesus, and he is subject to the Father. The Father and Jesus are over the Holy Spirit. The Word teaches this. The Holy Spirit cannot speak out on his own. He takes from the Father and Jesus and reveals it to us. He brings glory to the Father this way. The Ancient Scripts teach this. These Scripts have been kept by angels and faithful Jews through the generations. We have them revealed to us in this day. The Prophets and Men who wrote the Scriptures by Inspiration of the Holy Spirt got the very words of the Bible that are even in these Ancient

Scripts. The Holy Spirit is God. He is under the rank of Jesus. Jesus is under the rank of the Father. They are not of the same rank. The church that does not understand this has not had the revelation of the Father revealed to them when they read over the verses in the Bible. The LORD Father is greater than Jesus and the Holy Spirit. The Holy Spirit is to be worshipped. We sing songs to him. This is worship. Jesus is to be worshipped. We sing songs to him. The Father is to be worshipped over all, even the LORD Jesus and the Holy Spirit. The three agree, and this makes them one GODHEAD. We worship them as LORD.

## Let's Look at the Armor.

*"Finally, my brethren, be strong in the Lord and in the power of his might. Put on the whole armor of God, that ye may be able to stand against the wiles of the devil. For we wrestle not against flesh and blood, but against principalities, against powers, against rulers of the darkness of this world, against spiritual wickedness in high places. Wherefore take unto you the whole armor of God, that ye may be able to withstand in the evil day, and having done all, to stand. Stand therefore, having your loins girt about with truth, and having on the breastplate of righteousness;*

*and your feet shod with the preparation of the gospel of peace; above all, taking the shield of faith, wherewith ye shall be able to quench all the fiery darts of the wicked. And take the helmet of salvation, and the sword of the Spirit, which is the word of God: praying always with all prayer and supplication in the Spirit and watching there unto with all perseverance and supplication for all saints; and for me, that utterance may be given unto me, that I may open my mouth boldly, to make known the mystery of the gospel, for which I am an ambassador in bonds: that therein I may speak boldly, as I ought to speak."* Ephesians 6:10-20

Paul here explains that you are to put on the armor to be able to live this life against all the adversaries trying to take you out. You are to have the truth of God and his Word around your loins. You are to put on the righteousness of God. You are to live doing right. Your feet are to have on the shoes of peace. You were made to be at peace with God through Jesus' blood. You should know that you have peace and that you should bear peace as a fruit because of this peace and being led by the Spirit. The shield of faith is to have faith that God gave every man and even some an immeasurable amount of belief in God through Jesus Christ. In Hebrews, we learn that faith is the substance of things hoped for and the evidence of things not seen. You are to put on your helmet of salvation. Did you know that you are to be saved and have all the benefits that come with salvation? This includes deliverance and healing. When I put on my next piece of armor each day, I announce in prayer that I am putting on the sword of the Spirit, and I pray Scripture with that piece. Then, I move on to my prayer part of the armor. In this part, we are not just called to pray for ourselves but to pray for saints and leaders and pray in the Spirit (tongues). Paul asks for the believers to pray for him that he might have utterance and to speak the word of God boldly. This you can pray as intercession for the Apostle or pastors of your church. Though a prayer of intercession for someone, you could use it personally for you to evangelize with boldness and courage and the Spirit of God speaking through you. You must pray for the lost too. Paul is asking that he might speak to them and the saints. It states that we are to be watchful as people and for people and saints too. I am watchful. I know what the depths of Satan are doing to the church and nations and often know how and when to pray. You cannot do this well as a watchful Christian if you have no idea when to pray and what is going on every month under your nose, and you have never been taught about this.

# Watchful

There was a war in Heaven, and Satan and his angels were cast down to the earth. There are real angels that dwell in the heavens. Satan does go to and fro throughout the earth but has a kingdom in heaven (above the earth, not the 3$^{rd}$ heaven) and in hell. The ones on the ground working against you are angelic beings assigned to the earth that came from the angels kicked out of heaven. There was a group of 200 angels that made a pact to sleep with women, and they had children with these women. Read Genesis 6. The children were half angels and half human. They were called giants. These children were very evil. The angels that did this were called Watchers. In fact, angels, good or bad, are known as Watchers. The beginning of the bad angels was good. *"Now the giants, who have been born of the spirit and of flesh, shall be called upon the earth evil spirits, and on earth shall be their habitation. Evil spirits shall proceed from their flesh because they were created from above; from the holy Watchers was their beginning and primary foundation. Evil spirits shall they be upon the earth, and the spirits of the wicked shall they be called. The habitation of the spirits of Heaven shall be in Heaven; but upon the earth shall be the habitation of terrestrial spirits, who are born on earth. The spirits of the giants shall be like clouds, which shall oppress, corrupt, fall, contend, and bruise upon earth. They shall cause lamentation."* If you don't grasp this concept. Please read Enoch. If you don't believe Enoch, you have fallen to unbelief. If you don't believe Jasher, you have fallen to unbelief. There are people out there that dispute these texts and say that they are not the real thing. This is falsehood. The Lord preserved these texts throughout the Jewish nation and then put them forth for the world to read.

Now, the 200 angels who had children, half angel, and half human, went to hell and are bound there now. The evil spirits that were born half-human and half-angelic beings are on the earth and we know them as demons. Demons are not fallen angels. Fallen angels are the ones created from God that were kicked out of heaven. Their children that they bore are the ones that are known as demons. The LORD destroyed them in the flood but saved Noah and his family. The angelic beings that fell with Satan showed them how to oppress and hurt. The angelic beings that are in the heavenlies and on earth today go on and oppress. The ones that have thrones and reign in the second heaven are known as principalities and they are the ones giving orders to demons on the ground. There are demonic spirits that are down in hell that have orders there to oppress the people that are sent to hell after they die. They have this ability. If you don't grasp this, please read Mary K. Baxter's book. Jesus took her to hell many times to tell us about it. Satan and demons go there and take people there and lock them up. They go there and hurt people and have a circus event, too, in the place Jesus went to and rescued saints from.

The angels in the heavens give commands to ground demons on how to take over cities and nations and Christian brothers and sisters. You may not have been taught about what they are doing. So, I pray I can teach you something. I want to help you with being watchful in praying too. If something is on the ground, it is first natural then spiritual. Angelic beings that operate in the heavens do bury things in the heavens against us. In hell, Beelzebub is a ruler. Beelzebub was noted as a ruler of demons and a high priest of Satan. He rules them from hell to work horrible things on the people that are Satan's that go there. Jesus encountered him when he went there. He did not want to open up hell to let Jesus in. David spoke about this in Psalm 24. The conversation went like this:

*"Jesus: Lift up your heads, O ye Princes (gates). And be lifted up ye everlasting doors; the King of glory shall come in.*

*Beelzebub: Who is the King of glory?*

*David: I spoke of this Psalm. The LORD strong and mighty, the LORD mighty in battle.*

*Jesus: Lift up your heads, you princes (O ye gates); even lift them up, ye everlasting doors; And the King of glory shall come in.*

*Satan: I killed him. I fashioned the cross, the nails, the gall.*

*Beelzebub: This righteous man that has caused me trouble and brought Lazarus away from me. You brought him here? He rebukes Satan.*

*Jesus: I put Beelzebub over Satan for his words of rebuke to Satan"* [4]

You must learn how to reign on this earth from a position higher than the second Heaven. You allowed it to happen as a Christian because of your lack of knowledge in this area. Satan and the angels that were assigned to him were kicked out of Heaven, and Satan has been around for many centuries. In fact, they have been here for thousands of years. You have maybe been here for 20 to 100 years. They have an advantage over your knowledge, and they use it to defeat you. You live a defeated life as a Christian because you believe their lies and don't know how to outwit them in your mind. You cannot outwit them in the streets and cities either because of this. I understand this well. I have walked a defeated life. Satan lived with Jesus for many years prior to the replenishment of the earth found in Genesis 1:28. The earth was replenished from a prior state. See the very meaning of replenishment to understand this concept.

There are principalities. There are Rulers. These Rulers are like a King or Queen's power. I have heard of twelve principalities under Satan. The names are different in different languages. But from people who have dabbled quite a bit in witchcraft and have had personal communion with them. The names are revealed. The principalities are known by different names. These are evil ones. They were kicked out of Heaven by God with Lucifer. There are powers. The ground demons are territorial. They can be in anyone's home if allowed. Satan and demons can come into places. They are spirits. They can be kicked out too. But understand they can go throughout the earth. Fallen angels come through doors called Portals. Ground demons are the ones that are operating in the witches, wizards, soothsayers, high priests, generals, the bride of Satan (an actual woman Satan had sex with and is human), sorcerers, witch doctors, and warlocks. These human beings are people that astral project into churches, homes, neighborhoods, and even into your dreams with the demons when you sleep. It is easy for a non-watchful Christian to have a human being astral project into their home at night and even during the day. Witches and Wizards come into the church services if the leaders and congregations are unaware of this and how to stop it. But if you learn what is happening and know how to break it, you will be strong in the Lord and strong in the church. This isn't a joke. It really is happening. The witches are coming into the church building and putting things on you as you sit there.

The territorial demons are not just in the witches and warlocks. They may be and, in fact, are in or on bodies and souls. This can be why people are sick and dying. This can be why people are sinning so much. They have a demon that has been there through generational curses or by being sent to the person who is a Christian to bring them down. The ones sent came by a witch or warlock putting it on you to bring you down. You had no idea that a demon was sent to you because you don't know that the kingdom of darkness used a human being working for his kingdom to put it on you and to overpower you to lose what God has for you on earth. The demon might be there because of something you did in your past too. You had allowed it to live there when it came through one of your gates, and you don't know how to get it out. You got saved, and Jesus came to live in your spirit. But you still have a soul and body that has a demon or demons that need to be expelled. The demon may need to be expelled from your home or life.

## How to Fight from God's Heaven

Your position as a believer is not from the earth. Paul talked about the 3rd Heaven. God the Father has a Throne in the city of New Jerusalem in Heaven. You live on the earth now, but your home is in Heaven if you have accepted Christ into your life by believing he is Lord and God and came down to earth to save you from your sins. He died on the cross and rose again on the third day. Jesus is the second person of the Godhead. Consider there are three people. The Father, Son (Jesus), and the Holy Spirit. These three are Lord and called God. One God, One Lord, and Three Persons. The Father is Greater than the Son, and the Son is greater than the Holy Spirit. The Bible attests to this. Jesus told us the Father was greater than him. He said this as a truth. It is truth. He is not greater than the Father. I find lots of Scripture that attest to the reality of rank in the Godhead. The rank of the Godhead might be different, but they are ONE GOD. Since you received Christ, you now are a citizen of Heaven. God gives powers to his children. These powers are often exercised when the person receives Christ. You are able to operate in healing the diseased, casting out demons, and raising dead people to life. Jesus gave Christians this. Within the fivefold ministry, a Prophet is called to the authority he or she is given to pull down, plant, dig up, move in, build, bind, and loose. The Son, once he has reached 20 years, is supposed to enter into Sonship. Sonship has greater powers than the five-fold ministry over the Sun, Moon, and so forth and on earth. You can attain it before 20 years by being in prayer according to the Scriptures from 3 to 6 a.m. David took the wings of the morning. Jesus took the wings of the morning. Apostle, David Taylor, pointed out so many Scriptures to me that attest to this reality of meeting God in his time and not ours.

The territory in the heavens where the sun, moon, stars, constellations, meteors, meteorites, asteroids, and comets are needs to be prayed over too. The moon oversees a lot. It has the power to change the tide in the ocean if you don't know your authority or these operations up there. Then, you probably don't know how to fight for the people on the earth by watching to protect them. Satan and demons know, and they are putting storms on the waters and on the earth by your lack of knowledge and lack of ability to fight.

The power that the enemy campuses with the moon are to run operations according to the cycles of the moon. The moon has the new moon, first crescent, first quarter and terminator (half-moon), full moon, last quarter and terminator, and last crescent. It is for signs and seasons. This means that the LORD himself tells us and even the kingdom of darkness the season of the moon. If you are unaware of the things that happen at the full moon and new moons and even during partial eclipses and full eclipses, you are not fighting the battles that need to be won.

The warfare is in the heavenlies. If you are missing that fight, you probably are only fighting from the ground and on defense all the time against the kingdom of darkness. You cannot fight effectively and win this way. You need to learn the basics. At the basic level, the fight in the heavenlies is a big one. It is where the kingdom of darkness conducts what is going to take place on the earth. The LORD has given man signs to show him what season is taking place. The LORD has put the heavenlies in place to help us and to send judgment on us for the sins: iniquities and trespasses we commit. The Bible tells us in Genesis 1 that the LORD created the sun to rule by day and the moon by night. He tells us that he put the stars up there too. These illuminate the sky for us to understand the day from night. They have many features. The judgment of the eclipses themselves is revealed in Scripture. The eclipses and blood moon during a full moon reveal God's judgment. If we pay attention carefully to the things the LORD revealed to us in Scripture about the blood moons and eclipses, we will do better as a society to clean up our lives individually through the saving grace of the LORD. Jesus died to give us life, and that life is supposed to overcome the world. The world has a hold of so many people, including Christians. If we don't get in tune with the Spirit, we will never be able to overcome the sins we are entangled in. The enemy is smart, and he, fallen angels, and demons know how to manipulate us based on our own lack of knowledge.

There is an awesome understanding of the Scriptures. The LORD tells us many things about the sun and moon and their harnessing the earth. There are suns and moons that harness planets in the galaxies. Since God created this arrangement, he had a plan of what the sun and moon would be to his planets. They have powers. I want to exercise to you that this way of learning and use of skill can only come by God giving you galactical powers over these bodies. I told you that Sonship comes with powers. Some Sonship rights are over these bodies. Others could be by having mastery over water, like Jesus turning water into wine or walking on water. Now, if God gave you these powers to influence his Kingdom, your rights are to help people live and prosper and stop the kingdom of darkness with their witchcraft and sorceries. You know there are keys to understanding the fighting warfare in Psalm 91. In this Psalm, you learn of the times of day operations of the Kingdom of Darkness and the night. The Lord specifically tells you that at noon he comes to plague and kill, steal, and destroy. The Lord tells you that arrows fly by day. *"There are arrows that fly only by day. What empowers them is the Sun."*3

# How to Pray

Further, at specific seasons and cycles of the moon, you need to know what the kingdom of darkness is doing. There is a serious onslaught against Christians and the world during the new moon, quarter moon, and full moon. This is not the only time. I want to teach you just like I have been taught. There is an onslaught that you should know about during meteor showers, eclipses, and seasons that religious people celebrate and pray in the heavens about. This puts a heavy load on you, Christian, when you don't know how to fight in satanic or spiritual warfare during battles. You are always praying on the defense. Come on. Go on the offense and take it down in the Spirit. You need to pray in the spiritual warfare praying too. You need to pray it in the natural too. God doesn't expect to pour into you and not have you be able to be a strong Word Christian in praying in warfare intercession. You must get equipped with someone in this area. Why? Remember the armor piece of prayer? A lot of people stop at the Sword of the Spirit. They say the armor is a belt, breast piece, shoes, shield, helmet, and sword. But the last pieces are prayer and watchfulness with tongues of the Spirit. It tells you that you need to be a person of prayer, praying with petitions, intercessions, supplications, praying in the Spirit (tongues for all Christians), watchful, and praying that words might be given for the leader to speak boldly.

The armor is a personification of GOD to me. I come to you through Christ, my Lord. I personally have the blood of Christ to fight with and God to hear my prayers now. Christ Jesus has made way for me to the Throne of God. I have the Baptism of the Spirit and am filled daily. Shouldn't I tell the devil and demons to back off? I operate on a whole other level than you. I operate from God's Throne in the authority of Christ. You back off now! If not, I will take you down with my armor. I read the Sword of the Spirit, and I use it in prayer. The word of the LORD unto Zerubbabel echoes to us today. Therefore, the Spirit of the LORD is on offense with warfare. He sends angels when asked, and they will be on the offense with the Spirit of the LORD. The mountains that Satan, fallen angels, and demons bring before our lives are to become plain. Jesus is our headstone, and we have grace from God through him. This means our prayers are heard, and he brings favor to our lives.

*This is the word of the LORD unto Zerubbabel, saying, Not by might, not by power, but by my Spirit, saith the LORD of hosts. Who art thou, O great mountain? Before Zerubbabel thou shalt become a plain: and he shall bring forth the headstone thereof with shoutings, crying Grace, grace unto it"* Zechariah 4:6-7.

I pray with the knowledge that the heavens are very powerful, and the LORD indeed showed them to be signs. In fact, in Jasher, we learn that at the birth of Abram, the stars showed wonders. There was one star that came out of the east and then moved greatly and swallowed up all four stars from the North, South, East, and West. This means that Abram's birth showed the wise men who saw this that

Abram would be so great that he would conquer from all sides of the earth in his life. This was meant to be understood that his descendants would never be able to be conquered. We learn that from the Bible too. So, Jasher gave us great detail of this in the stars. What do I pray? I pray over the stars and the moon, and the sun. If the sun, moon, and stars give us light, then we should use what God gave us in our being to move the Kingdom of God with power on this earth and in the heavens. If God indeed gave some this power, it is up to us to use it. I pray using the blood of Jesus up there with the sun, moon, stars, and planets and all that is up there that has an impact on the earth and even beyond. I say beyond because there are planets and things outside our realm here on Earth. I want the kingdom of darkness to know that our God reigns, and I am not backing down. I face extreme attacks from Satan's kingdom because I fight so much up there with what he is doing. I am not going to share how much I get attacked but know that it is because I am part of the people that watch and destroy his works. He does great evil up there, and if we don't act, more people will die, and wars and things will take root.

# Chapter 5 - Regions

According to Satan, the territories in other countries and states in ours are to be controlled by principalities and rulers (kings) who have other authorities under them. The orders of those principalities are to be carried out by the demons on the ground called territorial demons and many names. The demons are after the rule in those states. In a mentorship by John, he stated the Principality is moved each year. How does that work? If we have different regions in the United States and we do. Just look at a map. Then, the regions are controlled by a principality. The Principality is a prince, that is operating under the guidelines of his rule in the heavens. He or she is ruling from the second heaven. They give orders to the demons on the ground over their territory. These demons carry out their plans. The Fallen One has ordered a military style of leadership. The regions in the United States are set up into five regions. The Ruler is a King Demon that can control a whole country.

Western Region: Alaska, Hawaii, Washington, Oregon, California, Idaho, Montana, Wyoming, Nevada, Utah, and Colorado.

Midwest Region: North Dakota, South Dakota, Nebraska, Kansas, Minnesota, Iowa, Missouri, Wisconsin, Illinois, Michigan, Indiana, and Ohio.

Northeast Region: Pennsylvania, New York, Maine, Vermont, New Hampshire, Massachusetts, Rhode Island, Connecticut, and New Jersey.

Southwest Region: Arizona, New Mexico, Oklahoma, and Texas.

Southeast Region: Arkansas, Louisiana, Kentucky, Tennessee, Mississippi, Alabama, Georgia, Florida, West Virginia, Virginia, Delaware, Maryland, North Carolina, and South Carolina.

In Ephesians 6:12, we are taught that we are wrestling against fallen angels and demonic spirits. The spirit beings are principalities, powers, rulers, and spiritual wickedness in high places. The demonic spirits report to Satan, who is the head of their administration and operations. The spirits I just told you cover regions. The United States is part of North America. Apostle Taylor, my mentor, told us that an Imperial god and a god are ruling the United States right now. You have powers that control finances and legalities. When one casts spells, they are working with powers. See the last chapter to see how they are using it in the schools.

They are asking the powers to cause a spell to come forth over someone for a specific reason. The person who knows witchcraft is communing with spirits in the realm of the unseen. Their faith is in a created being to who they pray and the demons who are controlling them. They work all this through demons who they are told to communicate with and to be held by a relationship of fear. They are told to put the fear spirits (called fear devils) on people the demons (gods of their worship) tell them to. All the while, they are held in bondage by fear. The witches pray to Satan, fallen angels and demons and see them. They are told by this kingdom of darkness to pray using thoughts to them. Did you know that demons don't hear your thoughts unless they put them there? The demons would only study you all your life to figure out your next move by the way you act and the way you seem to be to them by studying your character. They put their thoughts in your mind to take control of you by stealing your character identity as their own. The witches are taught to pray to their ancestors. Praying to the dead is witchcraft. They are taught to pray to the things of this world, too, like the trees. We will further this thought on the demons' controlling witches and warlocks and the people that are coming into your home and the church hurting you.

King demons are Rulers. We don't have a King in the U.S., but we do have leaders like a president and other leaders that can be influenced by demons and princes. Our leaders need our prayers. They are fully under attack by spiritual forces to bring them down and the states. The leaders are bombarded. They may have good intentions to help people. But if they are not Christians, then the state could suffer. If they are Christians, they need help to do what God called them to do for the people that are under their care. It is not right for us to put them down and call them names. Father says not to speak evil against them. We are to help them. If they are sinning and oppressing us, then we have to pray for God to show them the truth about what is going on in the spirit.

Demons are territorial. They want the territory of your family bloodline. They want what is yours. They want your town, your estate, your city, your state, and your country. They are fighting you to take over territory. They will not leave unless they are forced to. And often, some are wedged so thick in your bloodline that you cannot make them go without prayer and fasting several times. Why? Because we are a perverse generation. Jesus said, *"O faithless and perverse generation, how long shall I be with you? How long shall I suffer you?"* Matthew 17:17.

# Strongholds

**This tells you that the gang controls this neighborhood. You need to get this out of your town before your child is exposed to it.**

**The car on this train says Devils Night. It is an indicator of a gang. Gangs are graffiti masters.**

I want to turn to strongholds. The strongholds are real places those demons are worshipped, and these are the places in your city where demons meet to take down your city. They have their headquarters in your city where they can plan and go out to your street and house to take you down. If you do not curse these places and take them down, they will take your family down more easily. "Satan strategically plants strongholds in our neighborhoods, and every day we walk by the strongholds, and they become the norm to us... A demonic place where the devil meets with his people, yet we pass by it every day and brush it off like it's nothing instead of laying hands on it, cursing it to the root, and removing it."[2]

I have noticed strongholds of gangs. Hence, the shoe picture. This tells you a gang is in that town. This tells you that the gang controls this neighborhood. You need to get this out of your town before your child is exposed to it. If not, you could have people killed because you now have spirits of drugs and violence and fear and death in your town.

## Pray

*Father, in Jesus' name, I take authority over this town. I take authority from the north, south, east, and west. I now will take back everything that has been stolen from this town. I stand on the corner of this intersection in town to take back what was done in the spirit realm to take over this neighborhood. I break the blood ritual that was done to take this territory. I proclaim this territory is now Christ's from all four corners of the earth. This belongs to Jesus. I break. I smash. I uproot the curse on this neighborhood now in the name of Jesus. I break down the strongholds of this gang and the violence through guns, knives, and any weapons they are using. I break it down now. I break the bows used during the crescent moons. I break the swords of death and destruction at the terminators. I break the shadows during total solar eclipses. I break by the power of the blood of Jesus Christ all these things. I decree it is destroyed. I close every gateway and portal the principalities are using to come down here now. I shut the first and second heavens now against them and the ones on the ground, including Satanists and occultists. I tear down the spirit of intimidation, fear, drugs and alcohol, and the other spirits with these ones. I tear down the spirits of sexual immorality and the spirits of death now. I declare the people in this community to be saved. I bind Satan and his demons now by using mind-blindness to keep them from the truth. Tear down the false lies from their minds. I ask you to send someone to tell them the truth about Jesus. Send out the people of God to the people in this community. I declare that you will save them, and I call them back to the Lord. I believe though their sins are as scarlet, they will be white as snow. Though they are red as crimson, they will be as wool. Lord, let their iniquity* be pardoned. Lord, tell them you love them and draw them by your love now. Lord, these are your children. I fight for them to come to the Lord now. Lord, I love them. Lord, I want them to know you. Lord, let me speak to them. Lord, let them come to see what your kingdom and Bible are all about. Lord, let your love be magnified in their lives. In Jesus' name, Amen.

# Witchcraft Church

This is a church of witchcraft. This is a church that boasts all people welcome. Those that attend learn how to do witchcraft and live for Satan and demons for the rest of their lives. You will get possessed. You will get to do rituals and demonic things like astral projection here. They are a Metaphysical Church. The leader boasts of Christians attending here.

In this church pictured, I know of one that goes here and is on their board. She tried to love me and hug me. She tried to get me to let her do Reiki on me. I understand demons can transfer from a person that does witchcraft through physical contact of the mouth, and I believe it can through Reiki. I don't want a transfer demon. I said no. I understand Reiki is transferring energy to the body. I do believe that energy is important to the body. This is a fact. But in Reiki, the person is transferring energy from them to you. They are getting this energy from a long process of working on themselves. The energy they receive is through meditation and a process of improving themselves to know who they really are and to be happy in all aspects of life. The energy they receive from an outside source is from surrendering themselves to the Reiki power. Does the power come through alchemy pantheon gods? It could. I believe you are tapping into a source of the outside energy of the enemy. The Reiki Master is said to be learning all throughout life to get rid of the past and to have harmony for the future. The Reiki Master is working on getting the plan from inside of them for their lives. The Bible says the plan for your life comes from the Father, not from us. I know Christians use Reiki and state that if you believe in Jesus and the cross, that is all that matters. I have been told that the Father has ancient laws of nature. Reiki is not part of it. Everywhere I read about Reiki, it is said to be New Age Witchcraft. The people of this church and others like it want Christians to convert. I have the real thing. They can convert to Christ. Besides this, the woman loved me. I sat with her to get our makeup done, and we shared an interest in oils for healthy living. I know she uses hers in a different way than me; that is for evil and not just for healthy living. She wanted the same things I wanted in our inner man. We wanted to love each other and be kind. I know that when you get mixed up in the church of Satan, there is so much that comes in to keep you from the living God. I don't want her to be confused. The woman could have come to this makeup class I was at just to get other Christians and me into her witchcraft. I know this. Also, I have a woman I went to high school with mixed up in this church. I love her and want her to be free. I know if these two have understood me fighting to take back territory they worked to give to Satan, they misunderstand me and may believe I don't love them. However, this is not so. I do. But I will not stand by and watch Christians and families be attacked by demons because Satan told them to send them.

I have noticed the strongholds of Santeria. Santeria worshippers in your community mean that they are astral projecting in your homes and churches, and neighborhoods putting spirits on Christians and communities to take them down. I will go through many pictures and sort out these things in the rest of the book. One Santeria witchcraft stronghold was in the kid's treats shop. This is a place you bring children for a treat after school. But it is also a place where Santeria witchcraft is done. You might think you are treating your kids to afterschool treats, but you are exposing your children to Santeria. The shop is good. The Santeria worship in it is bad. I am happy the Lord gave the family a business; I want them to prosper. I just want the Santeria worship in it taken down. The people that run this place are equipped to enter your home during astral projection and change your life for the negative by obeying the demons and taking your family down. There was a god on a Pepsi cooler worshipped by giving it flowers. The god may appear as an idol to you, but in fact, there is more than one god Principality, to Santeria. The teachings, like Catholic teachings, explain the worship of saints. You are taught to pray to Lazarus and other Saints. The Lord has shown our generation that people are in hell for bowing down to Mary and the Saints. I used to bow down when I went to a Catholic church to Mary and Michael. The Lord showed me this was idolatry long ago, and I repented. If a Christian can go to hell for this, this needs to be renounced and repented of. I don't think Saint prayer candles are innocent. Did you know that one time I worked in a supermarket? These candles to pray to angels and saints were in the store. I didn't feel good selling them or working there anymore. I told a pastor I felt convicted after reading about the people in the Bible in Ephesus that came and threw away all their witchcraft things and burned them. I was told that God doesn't want you to quit your job and it isn't wrong for you to work there. Also, I had to get a liquor license to sell beer and alcohol. The same people came in every day and bought beer. Then, a worker at the end of their shift came through my line to buy liquor for a minor that worked in the store. I refused. I felt extra convicted about selling liquor and cigarettes. I would tell the people buying those candles not to buy them in my line. This is witchcraft. Praying to saints and angels is witchcraft. You agree with the principalities that you would rather worship the created than the Creator. So, I decided the pastor was wrong and quit. Along with this religion is spiritualism. The church of Satan is where most of these people attend church. It is not a place to hang out. There are real people in here that need Jesus. But know what you are entering when going in there. They are the ones Satan is using to take your family down at night. This church teaches roots, spiritualism, psychic ability, astral projection, ritualistic things to connect with the dead, and going into the graveyards to do demonic things. They teach you to learn about the principalities and make contracts with them to take down the people who are Christians. These people are not your friends.

# Chapter 6 - Take Down the Dark World in Your Community

First, you need to know that spirits exist. If you have seen decay in your city and county for a long time and in your prayers, you see little difference. You need to step up to the combat and take your armor and take your prayer life and watching life to an extreme. How? You need to get extreme. Come on. Get extreme. The enemy has been extreme and has taken over your city. In fact, I just moved to a city. I have been praying and taking notes. I was talking to someone in the supermarket that gave me a heads-up. The city doesn't even own much anymore. The Fire Chief and station are not in this city anymore. They were without proper funding to operate. I heard that I could not go to the town meetings and decisions be made in front of me. I was told that I would not be there when they made decisions. I was told that decisions would only be made when the residents were not in the meetings. I prayed for a new mayor, and we got one. So, what else do we do? How do we take back our cities? I need to first warn you if you enter this fight. You will fight. You will be fought against, and you will suffer. But there is power. There is power in our God and his Christ. There is power in the Holy Spirit. And we will break these demonic forces by understanding how to fight. But don't just go in to win. Go in knowing you have won. Because Christ has won, and you don't just defend yourself and the people. You go on offense in your authority. Your authority is not from Earth. Scripture says, *"And hath raised us up together, and made us sit together in heavenly places in Christ Jesus"* Ephesians 2:6

Did you hear that? You and I are raised together. We have power together. That power is better together and works better when together. So, I want to teach you to pray together in this way. This way, together, we will take back our families (homes), cities, and so forth. Even when we go to city meetings, the council cannot argue with God when we have prayed, and he decided on his answer. We are seated in heaven already. If we are seated there, our authority is there. We pray not from the Earth where demons and Satan are. We pray not from the first and second heaven where Satan, fallen angels, and demons are. We pray from the highest heaven where God the Father, Son, and Holy Ghost reign. This is above Satan, fallen angels and demons. We are in the offense position in the authority of his word, his

Christ, when we pray this way. Let's get going on the teaching.

I took the city I had just moved to and did an outline. There are strongholds in the city that demons hold. These demons are taking down the church in this city this way. How did I find this out? I was told by a source that one Baptist church closed, and now a mosque is opening in its place. How did this happen? Strongholds of demonic forces take over the city in the unseen realm.

**Let's look at my outline.**

# The LORD's Stronghold

7 Christian Churches, including 1 Catholic Church. These churches teach that you must be saved by grace through faith in Jesus Christ. They are teaching that there are three persons of the Trinity. Father, Son, and Holy Ghost are God and One. There are differences in doctrine, but they follow that the Word of God is authoritative and infallible. I have a lot of experience going to the Catholic church. I was led further into bondage going, because of witchcraft teachings. You pray to the dead. You light candles and pray to the Angels and Saints. This is done in witchcraft churches

too. Catholics would be wise to get this out of their doctrine and go back to the Word of God. All cases of talking to those that went on before us are not sins. If you try to talk to someone in your family at the grave. This is not a sin. I don't know if they hear you if they are not in heaven. But if you ever read the Book of Jasher, Joseph was calling on his mother at her grave when he was in distress. His mother answered him because he was crying and not wanting to go down to Egypt as a slave. God can permit someone to talk to you. I believe she was in the location of hell (Sheol) of Abraham's Bosom, and God permitted her to speak. Jasher said she cried out to him from under the Earth. The location of hell, called Abraham's Bosom, was under the Earth. It was separated from the part of hell that wicked people go to when they die. In Luke 16, we are taught that a great chasm separated Abraham from the part where one of his sons and others went who had done evil and not repented. When Jesus died, I believe he went down to Abraham's Bosom in hell. On the third day, he rose and brought them all with him. Some of them that died; the Bible said when Christ rose they came walking around Jerusalem. We have records indicating Simeon's sons walking around Jerusalem after they were resurrected. These are the sons of the same Simeon that was waiting for the Messiah. He was ready to die but did not depart until he saw the Messiah. His sons went on too. Next, these people went to heaven. They had to stay in Abraham's Bosom until Christ rose from the dead.

## Demonic Stronghold

# 8 Bar Listings

There was one within another location. The bars are places where witchcraft people go to find the worldly and to find the person who is a Christian who rides the fence and cannot figure out which side he or she is on. This way, the person can easily put spirits on you to take you down. Did you know that Christians drink? Yes. I am sure you know this. If you start to lose your sense of reality during drinking, you don't know that a person can play you because they were sent there to get you to believe their religion as truth. John Ramirez, once a warlock and general for the kingdom of darkness, told us during equipping us that he haunted bars to find Christians and to get them over to the dark side. I am not telling you never to drink. Kombucha can help your stomach. But drinking all the time is not good. I take probiotic supplements that don't have fermentation in them. Beer isn't all that good for you. If you are exposed to large amounts of ether, it will make you not well. I remember when I stopped drinking. I got tired of getting sick. There is Kombucha that isn't fermented. I don't believe that all drinking is bad. I believe in moderation; wine isn't bad. It might not be for me, but not all are the same on Earth. I am not the judge. People drank at a wedding when Jesus walked the Earth. He didn't have a problem with it. If you have a glass of wine or two at a gathering. What is wrong with that? I do believe God allows certain things. But to take it to the getting drunk thing and not to be able to not get drunk when you drink isn't good. Kombucha is good for the stomach, and if you don't drink but drink one of those, I don't see the problem. I don't want to drink because I want more of God. Suppose you are trying to get your stomach right. You need digestive enzymes and probiotic supplements. Once you get into taking these, your stomach is supposed to start lining up.

# 6 Liquor Stores

Did you know that the spirits on the ground are there because the principality in that year put them there to make the people drunk on alcohol? Therefore, you see so many liquor stores going up. Spirits referring to certain drinks have spirits attached to them. You haven't stopped them in prayer.

You haven't known why they are there. If the witch brings the principality into your region that year, and that principality happens to be like Delilah, a manipulator, and seducer, are you up to fight? You will know that your territory is being lost to the ground demons working for that principality. If you see poverty, then you have the principality that brought poverty that year. If you see homeless people everywhere, you have a principality that year that brought homeless people wandering everywhere. If you see a Jezebel like principality, you have a lot to deal with witchcraft that year. If you see a person sleeping in the church and community, you have the principality likened to Ahab that year. This is why you have not noticed the difference. You don't know what is going on in the city, state, and county you live in to take it down. So, the next year you are dealing with last year's principality operation. Now, you have this year too. We must wake up.

## 2 Smoke Shops

This is taking down the people in addiction and slumber. If fact, I am sure that many people are in a famine of the word of God because they don't read it every day but watch television and do their own likes. I am concerned that other demons come in. You could have infirmity demons come in because of smoking. They can put diseases on you.

# 1 Business to Bar Entertainment

This way, Principalities can take you over. This way, you can be sure your city is taken down. You can be sure that the bars that are entertaining the community through sleeping and slumbering and their own pleasures are not getting Christ and living an overcoming life.

# 2 Islamic Mosques

Did you know that a principality named Allah rules this religion? He is the god of the moon. When you go over to Muslims' houses, you will see they have moons all over their porch. Did you know that Allah is a principality of self-murder and dying? If you have these people in your community, they are held in extreme bondage. They are held in hate for Jews and especially Jewish women. They have a religion that is controlling them in ways the one true God never intended. I can't wait to show you about the moon. I am sure this principality of witchcraft isn't going to like it.

I want to talk about taking this down, but before I do, let me show you how I pray that I haven't had a good response. You may have been told the New Moon is about witchcraft and the Kingdom of Darkness. Get out of the Twilight books. You aren't helping but hurting. In the Bible and for the Israelites and Christians, the New Moon is prophetic. The kind of praying at the new moon is prophetic. The new moon starts another month. It starts a new moon cycle. The cycles for the kingdom of darkness are to take down the Christians and the world. The cycle for God is for many things. If you have Allah, ruling a people that are great and large, like Muslims, you need to know that they are praying to the moon god more than three times a day. And they are putting things into the moon through witchcraft that some are aware of if they are mystical Muslims, and some are not because of ignorance. The women in Islam are held in bondage through demonic forces in their homes, holding them in oppression and subjection.

During Ramadan, which by the way, is when we often celebrate the Passover and celebrate the Resurrection of Christ, there are serious evils being done in the unseen world. Let me show you a little bit of this so you can see why this is a major demonic stronghold in your community. The people in my community and county are numerous in Islam.

There are many mosques in the county. There are major sections of towns that are full of Islamic places. I was in a medical building, and I saw only Islamic writing on the wall. I thought I would be in trouble if no one spoke English. I cared because they must feel bad when they come into the country, I was brought up in a place where most speak English, and that is their second language. It must be uncomfortable.

Anyhow back to Ramadan. Muslims are known to observe the holiest night during Ramadan, which is better than a thousand months of serving Allah. The Quran 97:1-5 discuss Ramadan and the Night of Power. The funny thing is that the Quran is said in verse 1 to have never been discussed before sending it down. Thus, in my mind, Satan isn't smart here. The Torah was discussed before being sent to be written down. God gave Moses the Torah and Moses wanted it to be written down. We have Jewish records of it and long evidence in written form from Moses. The rest of the Bible outside the Torah was written down by the Inspiration of the Holy Spirit. We have a written record of Adam and Eve. We have a written record of Enoch's work. But here Satan works to fool a great and large people that the Quran was just sent down. It is said that Allah had it in his heart before the Creation of the world to send down the

Quran at just the right time. Muslims will tell you that Enoch, Jasher, and even the Bible are not accurate. They believe that we have corrupted them through time, and they cannot trust anything except the Quran as the actual Scripture. If I have learned anything in life, it is that you must look at things to see if they are accurate. If I never looked at the Bible and read it, how can I know if it is truly right? If I never touched the Quran to see what they are reading, how can I know if it is wrong? If I never looked beyond a news report to see the other person's side of the story, how can I know if one is right and the other wrong? I will say that there are things like Enoch and Jasher and many others that, if you have never read the Bible, you have no foundation to dig with to see if they are real or not. Plus, if you have not had enough study, sermons, and revelations, sometimes you don't get it either. I had a young Muslim man that I thought to help him understand Ishmael's life a little better by telling him about reading Jasher. He wasn't offended. But when I tried to tell him about Jesus. He went to my boss and tried to get me fired.

At the Night of Power, the Quran 97:3 says, "The Night of Power is better than a thousand months." The meaning behind this is that the Prophet Muhammad would forgive the person's past and future sins on that night of worship. The person is supposed to stay up all night reciting the Quran. Where did Satan get this idea? From Jehovah, our Christian God. He stole it. Jehovah actually revealed this to Moses in Exodus 33:22 in the meaning behind letting him see his backside to cover all his days. Then, to David in Psalm 23, that Mercy and Goodness would follow you all your days. Through Jesus Christ, all your sins are forgiven by Grace through Faith in him and the wonder-working of his blood. In Quran 97:4, it says, "The angels along with the Spirit descend in it by the permission of their Lord with all kinds of decrees." What does the Spirit mean? It doesn't mean the Holy Spirit to the Muslim. It means Gabriel. Why? They believe that Gabriel was viewed as Merited, Famed, Superior, and given higher Honor than others. So, the Quran is saying that Gabriel and angels come to the Earth this night to help the Muslims.

You need to know how to pray now during this time because if you don't, your city and county and state and country might be overrun. If you are not watchful during the moon phases and know what is happening up there and on the ground, you are not going to be effective. This year our president allowed the celebration of Ramadan in the White House. This has gone on since before Barak Obama. He did a festival. I was prophetically praying to break what was happing on the ground. Why? Because our president didn't know he was setting up our country to be taken over by a principality, Allah.

## What Do You Pray During Ramadan?

Watching is key. I have outlined before what to pray. Here in Ramadan, pray those things over the moon, stars, constellations, meteors, sun, and so on. But pray for more things too. If you have a tough time sounding shofars. Remember that the Shofar symbolizes the sacrifice of a ram instead of Isaac. It symbolizes obeying God's voice. This was the outline from the Old Testament of what Jesus would do for all mankind. This is an honor to God and Jesus for what he has done. It is an honor to sound the Shofar to honor God for his voice. Without Abraham, Isaac, and Israel, there are no Israelites. Without no Israelites, there is no Gentile Church. Without honoring Israelites, there is no honor for the Gentiles. Without honoring Jesus, an Israelite, we lack honor in our lives. Your voice to tell people about Jesus is an honor too. I believe using your voice as a trumpet is good too. Use your voice to honor him to lead people to Christ in salvation and through Kingdom gospel victory in their lives. This is a command to proclaim his testimony and blood.

Personally, blowing a shofar is hard. I usually have Jewish men who can blow it and sound it. This one isn't easy for me. I sound it at certain seasons from YouTube videos typically.

Pray for our President and leadership to be saved and stand for the Bible. Pray that our Muslim brothers and sisters will come into the Kingdom of God through Christ our Lord. Pray that people witness to Muslims. Pray that the Lord will show his power to the person you witness to that is a Muslim. Pray that Muslims will have dreams of Jesus. Pray that our leaders will have dreams of Jesus. Pray that the Bible will be the only Authoritative Infallible Word that is in our Government.

## Other Strongholds

I have taken pictures and gone into many businesses to see the demonic realm. I see that in places of business, the people are worshipping gods when the people of the community are not there. I have seen and felt the demonic strongholds when I go into their businesses. This could be a Chinese food place, or it could be a place where kids go for candy and ice cream. Let me explain.

# Occult, Including New Age Witchcraft

I am writing this section because New Age has infiltrated the church heavily. I am not happy with the way my brothers and sisters are being duped this way. One of the ways you are being duped is through the Essential Oils businesspeople. Essential Oils are beautiful to use for anointing if they have good names attached to them. I would not recommend buying ones that refer to your Inner Child Self. This is a demonic use of a name that demons use to put Buddhist principality beliefs on you. There are lots of demonic names given to food and things. You can overlook names, yes. Refer to Romans 14. Have faith. Further, witchcraft is not just to the Buddha's principality. It is through the Witchcraft Principalities likened to past Bible names of Jezebel, Delilah, Ahab, and the ones with Santeria and the ones with the demons that cover other religions. Anyhow, the point that I see my Christian brothers and sisters duped is through what looks like God is happy with you treating your body as a temple of the Holy Spirit and taking care of it by using Essential Oils that bring oxygen to the body and by the products sold by these companies that help you achieve good health. Yes, there are companies that have excellent essential oils, and the oils are used to help your body heal. Yes, there are good products that bring about the way that the body can fight a sickness attacking it. This is good. God did create plants and flowers and shrubs and bark to help us. The oil in itself was and is to honor the Holy Spirit. The Holy Spirit is the third person of the Godhead, and he is God. He is not, however, to be worshipped by worshipping the oil. The oil is not God and not the Holy Spirit. It is a created oil that was made from plants, flowers, shrubs, bark, etc., that God created. So, what you see in this is that Satan and demons have been around for thousands of years and know how to infiltrate the church, deceive the elite, and take them down by creating false realities. They are coming to you as wolves in sheep's clothing and telling you things that sound good and have Christian words or words that you would recognize if they told you how they used them in past generations. But they mask it with a new word to dupe you Christians into believing the witchcraft lies.

What does this look like? It looks like this. Chakras. You might have a check when I use this word. It is a check in your spirit from the Holy Spirit. You ignore this check and go further, and now you get duped by Familiar Spirits who follow you home and live in your house. I didn't say they were in you, Christian. But they can follow you home and have a legal right over you now. This is what you did. You had a Zyto Scan. You had a foot massage with oils where someone did a Vita flex on you. You had a hand massage where someone did a Vita flex on you. You had a massage where someone did certain things on you to manipulate certain areas using a technique that uses these methods. Now, if you ask these people to explain these things to you, they will tell you they are Christians and that they have seen many people get better by this. What they don't know is the enemy has set them up themselves. Spirits can transfer to you. The vita flex and Zyto Scan use chakras. Chakras are entry points to your body where demons can enter and exit. They can manipulate you to be feeling better and appear as if you were receiving healing. They often operate with infirmity demons. These demons you now gave legal rights to live with you and hurt you and operate in your lives because of your participation in these things. I heard a woman one time from the pulpit of a church where these meetings take place. You heard me right. I was wrapped up in this, you all. We had our meetings in the churches. Big Churches and we were taught from the pulpit. A woman said one time, I know the word chakra sounds bad, and she said it slow and drawn out to make fun. Then, she explained that she once thought it was bad but knows now it is a good word that was misused. The churches I am talking about are Christian churches and have the Baptism of the Spirit being taught. This is where we went for our meetings. Where you could get crystals and be taught about how to use chakras and how to use words of positivity to draw and attract people to you through the same beliefs as those in Buddhism. You would recognize a cat in a Chinese place used for good fortune and money, right? As a Christian, you might not recognize using good words along with your oils to attract money and people. These are demonic words that are spoken to bring people into your life. You are all the while duped the same way with demonic words used with golden or pink cats in Chinese places for good luck and fortune. This is not a joke! It is a legal right the demons have on you to afflict your life and destroy it.

Now that I have said all this. I have been advised that I am fighting against God's ancient laws about chakras. I have asked for different materials out there on chakras not being used for the demonic. But I have not been given them. So, I researched more. I found Christian beliefs that I was taught as a Christian on how they are good. I don't believe these things. This is what it looks like. The beliefs you see in the Witchcraft setting look like this. You are working with a Kundalini spirit, and this spirit has control of your spine.

This spirit seems to be what the people using Reiki are working with. It is a spirit that reports to Satan. Okay, so in the witchcraft world, the chakras open up points to your body so that you can feel better and be in balance. In the Christian world, you are told the Spirit of God is working with you through these chakras. You are told that the Spirit of God gives you revelation and wisdom. You receive the rainbow colors, and in your pituitary gland, you will receive the Lord helping you to have a sound mind. In your Pineal gland, you get revelation. In your thyroid, you get communication, and in your thymus, you get love. In your pancreas power and in your sexual organs, you get sexuality and abundant life in your adrenals. The Hebrew word for Chakra is Shakar. You are told that this word means dawn. In a Christian community, the chakras are justified by believing God is in it to bring balance.

Please understand what God means for the dawn is prayer. It is not balanced for chakras. The last watch of the night from 3 to 6 a.m. is for prayer to God when you can connect with him on the Earth and move in a greater power. He is Spirit, and he comes to Earth at this time in Spirit form. You are usually met with dreams at this time when he moves on the Earth. Jesus is often seen in dreams during this time. Further, I remembered a vision God gave a doctor. The organs are not for chakra entry points. They are to glorify God through Christ's sacrifice for mankind. In the vision, the doctor saw the organs representing what Christ did on the cross for mankind. There is Scripture in 2 Corinthians 4:10 that our bodies are always caring about the death of our Lord Jesus Christ. I know that this is referred to trusting God. Could it have a deeper meaning? Christians are being pulled down by Satan's schemes and wiles. He is changing words to get into the church and disable them and take their identities away. Please see below for more information on oils because you are not to dismiss oils and their qualities.

# Chapter 7 - Neighborhoods

This is a massage parlor that advertises as a health spa with a sauna. Yes, they will try to do massages on your back when you come in. See below what it is known for.

How did the problems in your city happen? There was a decline somewhere. What do we do about it? First, the Bible says to pluck up and pull down. It talks about God watching over you in ways to tear down strongholds and build up walls to defend you and to be in the offense position with the power of the Holy Spirit and the Word of God. The Lord often doesn't have an intercessor who is strong in satanic and spiritual warfare and a deliverance minister who knows how to operate to tear down things. This is so in many places all over the world. Therefore, how can God fulfill the fact of watching over you to build and plant? God promises in Jeremiah that he will send Jesus and bring a New Covenant with the people. The people who have Jesus are to operate at the warfare level for God to afflict, build, break down, destroy, pluck up, throw down, and watch.

*"And it shall come to pass, that like as I have watched over them, to pluck up, and to break down, and to throw down, and to destroy, and to afflict; so, will I watch over them, to build, and to plant, saith the LORD...But everyone shall die for his iniquity: every man that eateth the sour grape, his teeth shall be set on edge."* Jeremiah 31:28,30.

There is alcoholism in your neighborhood. There are people who are lazy and have no clue as Christians how to obey the Sabbath margin. Pricilla Shirer had an excellent study to learn about obeying the fourth commandment in the Bible. It is called, Breathe. I did know that we were supposed to not work one day out of the week, but it is so much more. I have even learned more about it since the years ago I did that study. There are people that are in your neighborhood that have declined and are growing more and more iniquitous. How did this happen? There needs to be someone who can operate to help the people. You must pray. Then, you will watch the Lord do something about it. He will if it is destroying the people. I have watched as I cursed a Jehovah's Witness Church that was beautiful on the outside and was in a prominent city fall. I cursed it to the root, and it went away. In fact, it turned into a Christian church. I cursed a Psychic shop to the root, and it went away. It turned into a dentist's office. There is the right thing to do, and this is it. There is the wrong thing to do. Nothing. You cannot watch generations of people fall because you didn't know how to pray and get it out.

There are people in these places that need Jesus, yes. You can reach them too. First, work to get that stronghold pulled down in their life. That building they are operating in is taking down your block and city, you know. The demons meet there and plot to take down the people on your block, and it goes out further. How? Just as I explained about Balak (also Balac), who was a witchcraft master who used witchcraft to take down the people of God, Israel. His history was long with Pharoah, and it stretched beyond Egypt. He went and lived in multiple nations and was advised of witchcraft. He was in Cush once, and Moses had to advise the people he pushed out on how to get back into their country. It took nine years. He was long against Israel. He knew God fought for them. This is what you learned in the Bible when he said I could do only what God says. This is because he had already seen God fight for them. Read the Book of Jasher. Sexual immorality and eating food offered to idols is the thing witchcraft brings about. It brings about you worshipping idols that you have no idea is an idol. It brings about sexual sins. It brings about division, anger, fighting, pride, and infirmity. It brings about you having a liking of someone at work outside of your spouse. It brings about you wanting money more than you ever had before in the wrong kind of way. Witchcraft done to you brings about the sins you are now stuck in and the iniquity (moral decay and even mental illness). This all happened because someone who knows witchcraft came around your neighborhood in astral projection and took it over and brought demons on the ground working under a principality to take you down. Why did that liquor store go up? Why did that bar go up? Why did that prostitution place go up called a massage parlor? The picture above is a place I have known for years. I remember around 2000, a businessman was at my home and talking with us. He mentioned that he and another guy went there and wanted the women for prostitution at night. The women said, 'We only do massages. But when the man and his friend pulled out money and cocaine. The women locked the doors and took them to the back.

Why did that church give over its place of worship to a group that wanted to do bingo and gambling at night? Bingo is known as lotto. There are other things than bingo the church is rented out for. They gave it over, and the people gave them money to be able to use their business for things outside of the place of worship and prayer God intended it to be. Witchcraft brought that about. Now, you have the Pastor who could be saying we need that money coming in. He or she could justify it by saying that all these programs and outreaches and electric bills get paid now because of the money that is brought in. Or they could say that we have all this space and are not doing anything illegal.

I hear of the things that are being done on the streets at night because the Pastor allowed this place of worship and prayer to be used as a space for a fee. I see it and hear it. Also, I have seen year after year in church rummage sales, people bringing in to sell witches and wizard stuff. I see Halloween decorations. I see a marketplace of selling things the store sells that are not for the church. Should you be selling things of Satan at the church? I was working one rummage sale at church, and a witch came in. I knew her, and she was surprised to see me. I talked to her, but she got out of there quickly. Do you know that they come in to spy and find things there for their own use? Further, they are there to put incantations on the congregation and the pastors. And they do. This might be why you are troubled when you are sitting there and even when you are up at the pulpit. She thought she could find witchcraft there. I knew other church members had put pricing tags on items to sell that were brought in that were direct witchcraft items. When they left the room, I took them home to throw away or threw them away when I found them. I even paid for them to throw them away. Churches also rent out space at God's house, the house Jesus called for prayer to thieves. Can God not provide for you? Let the King of glory in churches. But you have pushed him out.

## Cleanse the Church

*"And Jesus went into the temple of God and cast out all them that sold and bought in the temple, and overthrew the tables of the moneychangers, and the seats of them that sold doves, and said to them, It is written, My house shall be called the house of prayer, but ye have made it a den of thieves. "* Matthew 21:12-13

# God is Near

**I took this picture along with the next one. I was out working one
day, and God stopped me.**

What is going on in the natural brought this flag into the spiritual.
Love the person living here, talk to them, and care for them. Pray
for them. Curse the flag to the root. This is a stronghold in your
neighborhood. Curse the flag. God will ensure it is taken down.

I want you to understand that the people that do witchcraft and know it is witchcraft are coming out of their body through astral projection and do witchcraft at home and in the spirit out of their body to take you down person reading this. But Christians do witchcraft too. You do it in a dumb way. You don't get that is what you are doing because the ones who are real witches and wizards are bringing these things into your life to take you down. The reason is Satan and demons told them to attack you that way. And you didn't know because you don't see the unseen as they do. You see the physical and don't get what is being done to you in the unseen. They come in at night from 7 p.m. to 5 a.m. typically. They are taking territory when they do this. Let me bring you into understanding. This is what is happening in the spiritual realm and then what you see in the physical world (your life and in your residing streets of the neighborhood). They put you on lockdown. They lock a person, buildings, prayer life, etc., and use the force of controlling the people's ability to move spiritually in that area. This is now a very dangerous situation in which the Christians have found themselves. This disease has spread. They don't know how to get it out. You now have people who are into gay and lesbian sex in their community. There are drug addicts, alcohol addicts, prayerlessness, slumbering, laziness, and those who have fallen away from God. The reason this happened was that the Christians had no idea, and they did not pray. Maybe they prayed once, twice, or even more. But you need to realize this is being done every night. The devil, fallen angels and demons don't sleep, and they will possess someone who does witchcraft to come in at night to curse and bring the neighborhood or person down. If you don't fight and take the territory back every day or season, you have lost the battle.

As for the flag above, it is a flag that is called a pride flag for gays, lesbians, transgenders, and queer. Again, what is going on in the natural brought this flag into the spiritual. The people are living in a sinful way and the demons can do things in the spiritual easy to destroy. Love the person or people living here, talk to them, and care for them. Pray for them. Curse the flag to the root. This is a stronghold in your neighborhood. Curse the flag. God will ensure it is taken down. If you are not getting this and think I am putting forth hate speech. I will have you know the Bible tells you that the colors on this flag belong to the Everlasting Father (Gen 9:8-17). They are his colors from his own Spirit body. He is illuminating them from himself, as my friend Apostle Taylor explained. There are Scriptures that attest to this. Ezekiel 1:27-28 and Revelation 4:3 says, *"And I saw as the color of amber, as the appearance of fire round about within it, from the appearance of his loins even upward, and from the appearance of his loins even downward, I saw as it were the appearance of fire and it had brightness round about. As the appearance of the bow that is in the cloud in the day of rain, so was the appearance of the likeness of the glory of the LORD. And when I saw it, I fell on my face, and I heard a voice of one that spake. And he (Father) that sat was to look upon like a jasper and a sardine stone: and there was a rainbow round about the throne, in sight like unto an emerald."* Anyhow, I was on my way one day, and God stopped me. I remember having the feeling he was right there, and I couldn't see him. I said, 'Papa God, I haven't seen you do this in a long time.' I stopped and took a video and the above pictures. I started getting into my car and driving, and instantly, the rainbow disappeared. I believe God wants you to know he loves you. He wants you to know the truth. Satan used this to get people confused. Your mind was hijacked, and your sexual identity and identity as a man, woman, boy, or girl were stolen from you. Please don't think you should be ashamed. God takes all shame when you give it to him through Jesus. The blame is on Satan and demons, not you. I have sinned sexually too. I am not ashamed. God took that away. He will take it away from you too. God loves us and forgives us. He wants you to get your identity back. Demons have stolen it from you. The colors were for God to remind us that he wouldn't destroy us by flood anymore. These are his colors and from him. It is not something ever to be used for another reason. It is not for sexual orientation, and it is not for the leprechaun and gold. The Bible explains that it is his covenant token (sign) in the heavens for every generation that you are to live with him, and he will live with you and be your God. This token is prophetic. When I saw it, I was supposed to understand God called me to go beyond kingship to being called to spiritual emperorship. Also, he was saying to me that he was reminded of the covenant he made with all flesh to not destroy us by water. That is a good token. I want to go home to heaven when I die, and I know you do too. Even more I want to be translated. I want to stress again the heavens are important for signs. This is another instance where I am equipping you to pray into the heavens and over the earth what you see going on up there. God loves us. He doesn't want to see us destroyed. I am reminded of another prophetic time God made his point to me in the sky. I was working and looked out a window. I was struggling so badly right then. I was lost, and he put a cross in the sky. It was remarkable. I haven't seen anything like it since. He was calling me prophetic before I understood it. I know you have a call on your life too. It is for you to understand what that call is. I pray God will reveal it to you quickly. This way, you don't waste time on this earth not doing what he called you for. Prophetic is a priestly office, but there is something greater meant for your destiny.

My friend John Ramirez showed how the devil sent him to attack someone in a gay or lesbian-like lifestyle who did something that made the kingdom of darkness upset. "The devil is ok with so-called families, or people who are involved in homosexuality: Men living with men and women living with women. When it was time to do witchcraft on them, we didn't have to dismantle the family at all because they were already in sin. To teach them a lesson when they crossed the line against us, we would attack their bodies with a spirit of infirmity so they would die; because their identity was already stolen."[2]

# Chapter 8 - World of Satanists and Occultists

**That field is the world. It is the ground the Lord made. The seeds are the children that truly belong to Christ. The weeds are all around you. The devil has blinded their minds, and they are his children. But you need to know those weeds around you will grow if you don't help them be saved or fight against the wickedness that is attacking the people of God. It can and will not stop taking down you and your children and your families and your generations.**

What is going on exactly, Kathleen? The people who are high priests, root workers, sorcerers, warlocks, witches, and wizards are given commands by demons and Satan himself to take down the world of Christians. Christians are told to fight against Satan and his kingdom, and he doesn't like it because you are trying to take down what he creates and loves. You hate Satan, and the children of darkness love him. They believe Satan and demons love them. The demons take over territories through Satanists and occultists at night. The churches that do not fight back, which are many, are taken out of the fight in the spirit realm when a region and territory is taken over. The church has to grow into Kingdom knowledge and rule. Jesus has already brought the Kingdom to us we need to take hold and pull it down from heaven. The fight was unknown, and the people came in through a demon and flew over the neighborhood, walking around their houses and on their streets at night and did that. Do you remember the Parable of the Tares? It appears to me that when witchcraft was talked about in the Bible in many places, the people of God had no clue what was going on in the spirit realm. I want you to understand this is a biblical and spiritual way to come back to what really matters. You are in a war, and you need to know how to fight as a Christian of Jesus Christ.

*"Another parable put he forth unto them, saying, The Kingdom of heaven is likened unto a man which sowed good seed in his field: But while men slept, his enemy came and sowed tares among the wheat, and went his way. But when the blade was sprung up and brought forth fruit, then appeared the tares also. So, the servants of the householder came and said unto him. Sir, didst not thou sow good seed in thy field? From whence then hath it tares? He said unto them, An enemy hath done this. The servants said unto him, Wilt thou then that we go and gather them up? But he said, Nay; lest while ye gather up the tares, ye root up also the wheat with them. He that soweth the good seed is the Son of man. The field is the world; the good seed are the children of the kingdom; but the tares are the children of the wicked one; The enemy that sowed them is the devil."* Matthew 13:24-29;37-39.

# Idolatry

Let's look at a common one today. I want you to see this because this head of demons has spread nations and is taking over much territory in the United States of America. I took this picture at a Meijer store. It is a supermarket.

This is a stronghold in a neighborhood. You have a house on your block that serves a principality called Buddha. It is a stronghold that needs to be taken down. Breaking it and destroying it and dismantling its operation and cursing it to the very being of it there. This is satanic warfare, praying.

You have Buddha, the leader of demons, and others in this city.

Offering food to Satan and demons, idols, always have to do with idolatry. You are worshipping a spirit who eventually was made into an idol, a graven image. A graven image is something carved to form a god, and you would use it to represent the being that you serve. The graven image that is carved is typically made from clay (brick, earth, mud), metal (alloy, casting, ore), stone (gem, gravel, metal, rock), ivory (teeth and tusks of animals), plaster (cement and water or lime and sand), and wood (grove of trees or from trees). Now, you give that idol reverence by giving it gifts of food, incense, and flowers. You believe that idol is a representation of the person you are worshipping. Truly, you are worshipping Satan, fallen angels, and demons. Those individual spirits and demons took upon the identity of that idol to fool you. You hear of Bel, who is also called Marduk. This god was so influential that he fooled southern Iraq in the area between the Tigris and Euphrates rivers. Mesopotamia stretched farther too. The area stretched countries. It went into other parts of Asia, including Syria.

Let's look at a common one today. I want you to see this because this leader of demons has spread nations and is taking over much territory in the United States of America.

I took this picture at a Meijer store. It is a supermarket. The store wanted to rent space to bring people in and make money. 'Pull it down. Curse it to the root and get it out of there.' This is what I prayed. You betcha. I have seen it spread down the road to the Rite Aid in this city. I just started driving through this city. The other picture I took down the road further in the same city in a nice neighborhood. It wasn't an Asian family, either. Buddha can be in any house. The color of skin and culture means nothing. The person created in the image of God is why it is there to deceive and drag people to hell with the devil. In fact, I just talked to a Christian who told me that she once had a Buddha idol a friend gave her. She didn't want to give it up because a friend gave it to her. She said it took a long time to give up. The third picture was in a city in the same county. The principality demon is making its way down the county. Did you know that many Christians have no idea what to do? I know this because I have gone through the neighborhoods in this city that are large and seen from one neighborhood to the next the strongholds are numerous. The enemy did this at night, and it was done, and the spiritual warfare fighters were not prepared. I want you to be prepared. I want you to take it down. I want you to fight. I want you to know how. You have to have someone equip you. You have to stop sleeping and doing life for yourself. You have to fight. Your pastors are fighting. But you have to listen to them. Did you know that occultists pray in different principalities? One year you might have Jezebel. Another Buddha. Look at this. And did you know back in the store board game department at Target and Walmart, where the children buy their toys, you can buy a Ouija board or a Harry Potter game? Why did Buddha come in? Did you know you have witchcraft movies in the Electronics department? Did you know in another area of the store, you can buy sex books or books about magic or witchcraft at the stores your kids are walking around while you are shopping to buy groceries?

# Witchcraft Store

**This place is advertising to the people in this town that you can get healed and have the life you want back. You will get acquainted with your body, and the spirits of the occult will go home with you.**

Inside a botanica. This is a witchcraft store. They are advertising not only to their own people but to Christians and those in the community. I talked to a Christian in a business next store to this place. She had no idea this was a place of evil and to stay away from it. She thought you could buy candles and stuff there.

There is a psychic in here. They will tell you what you have done in your life and what you are doing now. They will tell you what is to come too. A familiar spirit came with you to tell the person about your life. A demonic spirit has followed you around in your life. Since you participated, a demon will go home with you and do all according to what they said will happen in time.

**The Botanica is named Faith and Love. This is interesting. There is the opposite of faith and love in this store and teaching. It is witchcraft.**

The store is telling you it has healing candles prepared. The Christian is confused because there is a Statue of Jesus and Mary here. This is witchcraft and idol worship.

Not today, demons and Satan. You are being exposed.

Catholics, spiritualists, and Santeria could be among the people shopping here. I stood and watched to see who was going in one time.

There is a medium in this store. If you want a witch to have control over your life, shop here. This is a place where you are going for healing, they tell you. But what you are going to is a place of learning about the deep things of Satan. You will learn this, and you will not be healed.

Inside a botanica. This is a witchcraft store. They are advertising not only to their own people but to Christians and those in the community. I talked to a Christian in a business next store to this place. She had no idea this was a place of evil and to stay away from it. She thought you could buy candles and stuff here. There is a psychic in here with familiar spirits. They will tell you what you have done in your life and what you are doing now. They will tell you what is to come too. The reason is a spirit came with you to tell the person about your life. The spirit will tell the spirit in this person what they have seen in your life and what you are doing right now. Since you participated, a demon will go home with you and do all according to what they said will happen in the time to come through the voice of the psychic. These places are advertising to the people in their towns that they can get healed and have the life they want back. You will get acquainted with your body, and the spirits of the occult will go home with you. Inside the Botanica, you are enticed as a Christian to come to the other side. You buy oil and believe it is the Lord's will for you to buy this here. It is a trap. You are trapped with the purchase. It is a demon that is enticing you to buy from the witch's place and their oils instead of buying it at a credible place. Now, the witch will astral project to your home and infiltrate your life and family. Inside the Botanica, you can learn about roots. These roots work with ancestral strongmen in your family bloodline. These are workers of spirits in the heavens. There is a flyer on the store door. It is enticing you to come to a festival and have entertainment and food. You are entertaining with the kingdom of darkness here. You will go home with a demon if you attend.

# Voodoo, Hoodoo, and Roots

**Inside the Botanica, you can learn about roots. These roots work with ancestral strongmen in your family bloodline. These are workers of spirits in the heavens.**

This is a flyer on the store door. It is enticing you to come to a festival and have entertainment and food. You are entertaining with the kingdom of darkness here. You will go home with a demon if you attend.

The Horror pictures on witchcraft, like The Conjuring and Candy Man, are Voodoo and Hoodoo. You are working with very strong men in your family bloodline. This was taught to me as a child by my neighbor. They would have me watch horror movies. Then, they would have me go to a graveyard and at home to conjure up the dead spirits. I didn't tell my parents. I wish I had. I was only a child.

The workers of roots are using methods of divination. This way, they can call on the ancestral strongmen in the heavens. These strongmen rule your past, present, and future. You are locked by gates in the heavens during certain seasons of your life. This happens when you are born through transference, every year you age, and so forth. This is the knowledge that you need to get things out of your life. We have the power to break things in the heavens. And there are times to go to the gate and take possession.

You often hear a word called Mojo. This isn't a good word. You hear artists singing about Hoodoo and Voodoo on the Rock Music channel. You sing along. Did you know when you listen in your ear gate and open your mouth to the songs of the world music like this, you have given Satan legal rights? The LORD is serious about you giving him your gates and getting deliverance from the gates you entertained demons with. What is on your head? Your ears, eyes, mouth, and nose. What is in your head? Your mind, will, and emotions. Is your spirit man in there too? Can one get access to your body through your head? You are created forever. You will either live with him or with Satan for the rest of your life. He wants you to live with him. He is explaining your gates belong to him, not the enemy. So, be wise and choose Jesus for salvation.

# Essential Oils

Inside the Botanica, you are enticed as a Christian to come to the other side. You buy oil and believe it is the Lord's will for you to buy this here. It is a trap. You are trapped with the purchase. It is a demon that is enticing you to buy from the witches' place and their oils instead of buying them at a credible place. Now, the witch will astral project to your home and infiltrate your life and family.

Let me tell you one thing that witchcraft people often understand better than the body of Christ is the use of these for the body. Why? Satan took what he learned from God, manipulated it, and used it for his people to tell them how to care for their bodies properly. Yes, good essential oils do, in fact, heal bodies and do it well. It is a way of taking care of the temple of the Holy Spirit. Again, I don't use Chakras. I use my oils to put in veggie caps or in water. I use them to make anointing oil. I use them to smell in a diffuser. I use them to make deodorant. I use them to make good cleaners mixed with water and other things I mix with it like baking soda and stuff. But we (even me) often resort to using the medicine on the shelves called Tylenol, Motrin, and such or the pharmaceutical prescribed medicine. These medicines are made of constituents (natural) of little to or up to 20 ingredients. In contrast, essential oils are distilled properly and made from organic, non-sprayed, with harsh chemical ingredients like plants, shrubs, etc., of constituents up to 100 and more. This is why you experience great maximum healing effects more quickly.

The pharmaceutical drug is made of petrochemicals. A petrochemical is obtained from under the ground. It is not such a good thing. It has a petroleum base. Can you see why God would use essential oils mixed with fatty oil to bring healing to people? Can you see why the oil often referred to the Holy Spirit in the Old Testament? The person of the Holy Spirit is God. He is part of the Godhead. He preceded Jesus on this earth. He lives inside the spirit of a Holy Spirit baptized believer of Jesus Christ. Jesus also brings the Father with him to live in us. I read this in the Word under Sonship rights. The Word of God says, "If a man loves me, he will keep my words: and my Father will love him, and we will come unto him and make our abode with him." The Holy Spirit is the one who works in us on this earth through his fruit and through spiritual gifts that bring honor to the name of Jesus Christ. The Holy Spirit is the one that moves us to do the ministry of Christ. He heals with Christ's workings through us. We have him in us to bring healing and deliverance to the people in this land and to the lands the Lord sends us to.

The essential oil is very much anointing oil if it is distilled right and kept right. I use them, and they bring oxygen to my body. There are wonderful things I have witnessed in my own life by using the right ones. I have tried many. I have known the good from the bad. Believe me; there is so much bad in the market that people are deceived. Did you know that there are fragrances so much in products that cause cancer? I have been in the health realm with oils for years. I can counsel you that if you buy Tide or the main brand, you are exposing your house to cancer. If you buy the main brand and colognes, you are exposing your home to cancer. There is a knowing in my home. I live, yes. But I have walked the walk with this stuff to see it is killing our generations since the latter 1900s because Christians are buying it and not getting it out of the homes and churches. I am telling you the truth. The back information that I see from the companies is that there are laws that are grandfathered in the United States that these companies don't have to tell you the amount of fragrant (cancer-causing) ingredients in their products. I see the health realm that there are more people getting cancer for the fact of the environment in the home than from their ancestors. Generational cancer is less than 10 percent, while environmental cancer is the other 90 percent. This is sad. I can tell you much more. But I want you to know that the enemy has sent demons into the Christian home to take them out this way. The oils that are pure and right smell and taste different. They are not watered down and mixed. There are other brands and products I see and have tested. I mention products in our homes because these products have so many fragrances in them that are messing with people's bodies and causing diseases and generational diseases. They are harmful to breathe and use. I was just in a kindergarten class where the kids cleaned with Lysol wipes. I was instantly sick when they started using them. The essential oils now put in lots of products might not matter if they have other stuff mixed in with them. I walk this earth too. I work really hard to make my own products for the home or buy healthy ones. Do I mess up, and do I still live? Yes. But I am getting better and working on getting things out. I have been doing that for a long time. God is continuing to help me. Candles are awful if they are fragrant and can cause much harm. I have seen pictures of children hurt by candles and products.

Anyhow, the Holy Spirit has good oil, and it is even depicted that way in the Bible. It is not bad and wrong. It is right. Therefore, know that Satan and demons use the oils for their people, not only caring for their bodies but for the spells and magic they perform. I want you Christians to know that Satan didn't get this and use it from his knowledge. He took what he saw God use and now performs evil and weird things with it. Please understand I know a lot about this. Do not get the books on essential oils and perform them to use for doing Yoga and Meditation. This is diabolical and will allow a demon to enter you. This will do this. If you fall into the trap here, you have allowed the devil to convince you of falsehoods. Also, they use it for the workings of chakras. The

Christians are going for treatment and thinking it is helping, but you are getting demons to afflict you now. The massage therapist that has learned the terms of vita flex (modernized term) does not understand that this was designed to afflict mankind. These are terms long used for chakras. This is the occult. You are working with the kingdom of darkness now. They have modernized the terms to fool Christians. It is still the same enemy. He is smarter than you in a lot of ways. He has been around for thousands of years. He was even with the Lord Yeshua before the earth for those years. He was here when Adam and Eve were created. He is working against you in a realm you might not know about. This gives him an advantage over you. He is working in the ways that he was taught but uses it for the evil of his own heart and desires to kill, steal and destroy you.

You might hear Christians in this circle who are using these terms, and Reiki say certain things, like we were taught to use it for the glory of Christ, and we see it helping the people. This is what I hear Christians say to me when I question such things. You see, the enemy is deceiving you. Did you know that he comes with his powers to heal too? He was created by God with powers that are different than ours in strength. The angels were to minister to the people. Now the demons use it to show you healing in your body. They stop afflicting you. This seems like the chakra vita flex and Reiki is working. But what you don't see is the demon is now with you. He will come and afflict you with disease and sickness again. He is with you now. The Bible talks about the enemy coming with the power to heal and work miracles. This is false healing and miracles. You are deceived. You have met the occult and now have opened your soul and body to demons. If you are a Christian, you need deliverance. You are into witchcraft. This is a long-time ago thing and read throughout the Bible too. The enemy deceived the people of the Lord by bringing them around the witchcraft people who knew what they were doing in secret. They fooled you. Or maybe a Christian fooled you who had no idea about these things. I grew up with neighbors into witchcraft. I did a lot of things unknowingly, and this is because I was a little kid and didn't know better. I didn't tell my family either. Then, Christians fooled me again. The devil is using the same things to fool us over and over again. We have to wake up. I use essential oils and good products. I just don't buy everything that has the name inner child, higher unity, or magic on it. Specifically, those were given their names from Buddhist practices of higher unity to get to be one with self and to connect to your inner child. These are designed to fool you into those practices of Yoga and meditating with demons. These demons enter your body and soul. I separate myself from people that are working in these things that I got out of. I saw. I did. I overcame. I am not going back!!!

## ITOVI and Zyto Scan

Satan is very mischievous. Did you know that ITOVI and Zyto Scan have made their way into Christian circles? Satan didn't just tell you upfront; it uses chakras. He dumbed you down. He told you it would help you to use this as a natural way to find out what your body needs and what organs are messed up. It uses chakras. Then, you get dumbed down when you see it tell you exactly what the doctor has told you before when you get your scan. Did you know demons are there when you get your scan? They know what is going on with your body. They manipulate the scan to be able to enter your body and soul and live there. Chakras are not good. If you have been told this is okay. You were lied to. You now have been operating in witchcraft. This is advanced witchcraft. You have demons manipulating your body and telling you what you need. This is occultic. You have opened up to the occult. If you are doing this, you need to repent and renounce and have a deliverance minister help you immediately. There are spirits oppressing you. I used to do this. I was dumb. I taught this for a long time. I didn't know it used chakras. The machine works by telling you what your organs are doing, your hydration, emotions, and so forth. You get demons manipulating the chakra entry points into your body and soul. You need to get them out. They might help you feel better by not afflicting you as much some days to lie to you. But the truth is that it is a setup to kill you.

What are you talking about? I am telling you the truth. You don't see the unseen. You don't hear the demons or Satan unless you have opened yourself up to having conversations with them and seeing them. I was introduced to witchcraft by a neighborhood family. This family, at an early age, led me to understand and do witchcraft. We did light as a feather for real. But what I want you to know is that God has deliverance. God has everything you need. You don't need demons. You don't need Satan. You need the LORD, who is Jesus, to set you free. If you have Jesus, you have overcome the enemy. But you still may need deliverance because of generational curses, things you entertained and have done, as you were led captive by spirits.

# Christian Witchcraft

There was a conversation in secret. How do we get into the Christian circle to take over what they have? The same conversation happened with Balak, the King of Moab, and the expert in witchcraft, Balaam. Balaam showed him how to seduce the Israelites to get them to leave their God. The same God who delivered them and carried them through. This is what is in the market of America today. This is what has happened to Christians. Christians were seduced by an expert in witchcraft. They showed them they could get rich and be healed. They showed them that they could have the things in life God wanted them to have. All Satan had to do was change names and put God the Holy Spirit in the mix of it. He seduced them on their own terms. He seduced them with his terms. He just changed names and had the network of witches and warlocks go about the church. Then, he let the church spread the witchcraft to the church body. I know. I did it. I am so sorry to all the church members I have hurt. I didn't understand what I was doing with Zyto Scans. I didn't know. I pray you will forgive me. I led many classes. I instructed many people. I had checks in my spirit. I did; I wish I had listened to them immediately. I fell for it too. Christians seduced me by the enemy seducing them.

I still use good products. I do. I believe in taking care of my body. But I will not use the furthering of the kingdom of darkness anymore. A good product is a good product, and that is it. The enemy is using God's oils for manipulation. I don't buy them in the Botanica. I am very angry with the furthering of this sickness. I like the products that are used with good processes and organic materials. But to call them names that are foolish and to take what God meant with Jasmine and Lavender and so forth and use witchcraft terms and beliefs is sick.

# Yoga

**This is a location that many people go to. This is everywhere on Canadian T.V., but it is all over the United States too.**

I wanted to mention that I had a woman at church get upset with me because I tried to teach about this on my Facebook page. She was upset and said that she uses Yoga with her daughter, and it helps her body feel better. She stopped coming to church soon after and took me off her Facebook page. I share about this experience and share again that I have walked this. I did Yoga in my 20s. The only thing I got was a lack of peace. I will hear Christians tell me, Kathleen, I don't do that type of Yoga. I exercise. No. No. No. You are deceived. I did Yoga. You get demonic spirits attached to you. This is from the devil. I don't care if you hum, breathe, or exercise Yoga. It is all the same. You are meeting demons. These demons have a game plan to seduce you into thinking it is okay. These are worldly ways that you are seduced into. I have a lot of experience in the witchcraft realm. I have seen demons, talked to them, and seen them appear in human form. Also, I believe I have seen God's angels come in human form too. One encounter was after a demonic spirit appeared in human form. The male demon stood very tall. I was driving, and I got on an off-road. It was snowing heavily. The demon told me I had to go to the right. The next thing I knew, I was stuck in the snow. No one was around. It was really bad out. Then, three angels appear in human form to help me. They pushed my car out of the snow

I was stuck in, and then I couldn't see them anymore. I have had good angels help me at other times. I have been in serious bad situations where I should have died, and they showed up. I have seen demons in spirit form too. I know a little more than you about this subject. You are getting into trouble if you entertain Yoga. It is not for your exercise. You are putting your soul into vexation, and your body will be exposed to demonic forces to put you into an infirmity if you entertain this Yoga into your gates. You have given access to your gates to Satan. God tells you that your gates belong to him. If you have opened them to spirits, you need deliverance.

# Chapter 9 - Generational Spirits

There are several things on draft. There is a ritual done here. It may appear innocent to drink here. But you are deceived. I will expound further in the next pictures.

This is enticing to people who love free stuff. First, if you don't know about Halloween as a Christian or think it's all about the candy for kids and innocent. You are fooled. The person here allowed me to ask her several questions. I was able to get down low on the demonic ritual that Christians, witchcraft people, and the community can do. The ritual involves several drinks and food if you can't stomach all the drinks. You are doing a ritual and making a contract. You don't understand what you are doing if you think this is fun and you get a free shirt.

3 Floyds are known for witchcraft. If you think comic books underground and zombies are okay as a Christian, you are deceived. Zombies are, in fact, what some look like. The LORD changed their form when they fell.

The bar shows you that there is a fridge full of various beers. There is on draft many strong beers. The ritual is to drink ten beers. The bartender mixes seven 12-ounce beers on draft and three 12-ounce beers in the cooler. You have to drink all ten to get the shirt. If you choose, you can pick seven beers from the bartender and three items on the menu to eat too. You make a contract by doing this ritual. You are now legally his. He has legal rights with you, and you will operate under his influence. There is a court in heaven, and Satan will tell God he has legal rights over you. The demon that goes home with you is a spirit. The contract is with a Principality, and a demon is now with you.

There are several things on draft. There is a ritual done here. It may appear innocent to come here and drink like this. But you are deceived. This is enticing to people who love free stuff. First, if you don't know about Halloween as a Christian or think it's all about the candy for kids and innocent. You are fooled. The person here allowed me to ask her several questions. I was able to get down low on the demonic ritual that Christians, witchcraft people, and the community can do. The ritual involves several drinks and food if you can't stomach all the drinks. You are doing a ritual and making a contract. You don't understand what you are doing if you think this is fun and you get a free shirt. 3 Floyds is known for witchcraft. If you think comic books underground and zombies are okay as a Christian, you are deceived. Zombies are, in fact, what some look like. The LORD changed their form when they fell, according to the Ancient Scripts. The enemy and demons can appear as an angel of light, but the fact that the LORD changed their appearance to be ugly is still the same. The bar shows you that there is a fridge full of various beers. There is on draft many strong beers. The ritual is to drink ten beers. The bartender mixes seven 12-ounce beers on draft and three 12-ounce beers in the cooler. You have to drink all ten to get the shirt. If you choose, you can pick seven beers from the bartender and three items on the menu to eat too. You make a contract by doing this ritual. You are now legally his. He has legal rights with you, and you will operate under his influence. There is a court in heaven, and Satan will tell God he has legal rights over you. The demon that goes home with you is a spirit. The contract is with a Principality, and a demon is now with you.

These are typically generational spirits in the bloodline. You have here things locked in the heavens with ancestral strongmen about your bloodline. Somewhere in your bloodline, you have had witchcraft or alcoholism that brought you to be set up to do this ritual. The enemy got you where he wanted you to put the hook in to continue on down your bloodline to do this work. Another possibility is a transfer spirit. You are in a sexual relationship with someone with these types of demons, and you were exposed to this through that person. You may have had a transfer demon come through your encounter sexually with that person. The transfer demon may have been an alcohol demon.

# Spirits of Alcoholism, Drugs, and Mammon

**These are two businesses side by side. You have spirits of alcoholism and drug addiction on your block now, along with the spirit of mammon.**

This place tells you it sells spirits. This is not just an alcohol reference. It is a demonic people who are called spirits of alcohol. They have this assignment: To go home with you when you buy these drinks and drink them in places. They go home with you because you believe the lie that you are just getting drunk or having fun for the night.

Drug and alcohol demon stronghold in this city neighborhood. I
have in a mile or two stretches on one road several bars,
recreational drug shops and liquor stores, and Santeria witchcraft.
I believe witchcraft has a big part here.

**You have demonic strongholds of alcohol and drug addiction here.**
**You have a love of money (mammon stronghold) here.**

**The Principality is announcing to you that it started as a weekend smoke or when out with friends like a teddy bear you seemed to be able to control. Then, it becomes a dragon that takes you down.**

You have allowed this city to be taken over. Recreational is big on this road. This is a long stretch of road in a certain city that has many Recreational marijuana shops (Drug spirits). I see many spirits have taken over this city and county and have been allowed to have free reign. Ahab, Jezebel, Delilah, Vagabond, and other drugs, alcohol, witchcraft, and poverty spirits.

I know there are a lot of CBDS out there. There are good ones. But, I have seen a lot of it has things mixed in it that are not good. Perhaps, all the THC is taken out, but the thing mixed in it isn't good.  I have heard people say that they don't have marijuana send them into a hallucinogenic state, while others do. I see. I understand there are a lot of sick people out there. Our deliverer, Jesus came to set us free from all bondage. I am not trying to condemn anyone. I have demons I am still trying to break free from. And not one Christian can say they don't encounter attacks from Satan and demons. This is just not the case. Further, the more you do for Christ you will get attacked. If you are not being attacked, it is possible you are not a threat to the kingdom of darkness. If you do work like this, expect the attack to be heavy. In fact, it is very great. But my God is stronger. I just know that Satan is smart, and if he can get someone into addiction, he will do it. There are certain spirits attached to certain things. Some are attached to recreational marijuana, while some are attached to pharmaceuticals (pharmakia spirits). Recreational marijuana is for partying to get high and have fun. I don't personally understand smoking marijuana. It seems to be not good for the throat. I would think cooking it would hurt less. But as I understand, just because it is legal to have a recreational hobby of marijuana partying in America doesn't mean it is God's will. We all need help. We all have issues God needs to help us with, and that is just what happens when we come to Christ. Then, ask for the Holy Spirit. The Holy Spirit starts working on us to make us like the LORD Jesus Christ. We don't come without sins. We come with them just as we are. If I could explain what I was like in so many sins. It wasn't as if it was pretty, and I didn't do wrong. It isn't as though I haven't still sinned since, either. God is still working on me.

We could use our bodies as not intended in a sexual relationship, married or unmarried. We can use our mouths to speak evil against one another. We can shed hate with our mouths and actions. We can be murderous in mouth and workings. We can commit great sins of witchcraft with cannibalism and such. However, Jesus took every one of them. He did this for us to be with God forever. The Lord did this to make our lives righteous. We aren't righteous. He is. We are his righteousness, and the Holy Spirit will work in us to make our minds and thoughts like his.

The spirits that are attached to these places of lotto, beer, wine, smoke shops, and recreational marijuana need to be kicked out of our neighborhoods. We need to bring them down. They are taking down our lives, families, children, and communities. We have to care. If we don't, they will grow. This means we have generations of children growing up with people teaching them that these things are okay. Then, they instruct their children they are okay. What happens next? God's judgments. God does judge our evil. California fires and storms come, and things like the coronavirus. He judges us for our evil. We listen and let him change us, or more people die. When a person dies, they either go home or to hell. There is no purgatory. There is no reincarnation. There is no second chance. If fact, this is our chance. Listen or learn by lesson. I remember a former Texas pastor named Donny Granberry, teaching me that. He said in a sermon, you either listen by listening or you learn by lesson. He tried to help me. He saw I was messed up by the Catholic church and by many things.

# Chapter 10 - Spirit of Mammon and Sex

This is a naked women club. They offer you prostitution, sex, music, and drinks. Little do you know when you go here, you are now followed home. You may have come here for fun. But you are likely to leave with a husband spirit, wife spirit, incubus, succubus, lesbian, or gay demon.

Here I am at one sex club parking lot, looking over at this other one.

Looking beyond this big sign is Velvet Touch. It is a chain. You can buy sex toys and movies. There are women waiting in a room too at the front for sex. Across the street, you have the Z Club, known for homicides.

This place is a sex club. It is operational all week, and they are enticing people. Beyond this place used to be the State Bar. It was a gay bar for men. Now shut down. Praise God!

This is an adult porn shop. When your people get sucked in here in the community, it will take years to get these demons off without a proper deliverance minister in your church. They will be the people like the witchcraft people who are bound by sexual sins. But the demons in witchcraft have brought you into more witchcraft through this. Astral projectors have put your community through Principalities like Molech into heavy sexual and witchcraft demons.

This is another shop to buy adult movies, clothes of sexual fantasy, and sex magic objects for use in witchcraft. Tantra is witchcraft.

This place is a shop that sells sex items. It includes items for sexual perversions and videos. These are places in the community where once your people get into this world, it probably will take them ten or more years after coming to church to get the demonic effects off them. This place is a disgrace to Adam and Eve, our forefather and mother. It needs to be cursed and brought down by knowing how to pray.

I am reminded of hearing someone preaching recently that when a man came into his church and said he had a ministry going into the sex club to get people out, he told him he was mistaken. He said God would never use you to go in there to minister Christ. I am not saying he is wrong. But what I am saying is that God is everywhere. He is right there in the sex club, just as he is watching you in the church. He can and does use people to get the people trapped in these places out. Let me explain. I have noticed that the people that own the bar, witchcraft store, or such usually live above it or are attached to it. These people hardly ever leave it unless it is to run to the store to buy milk when they need it to mix drinks. I know this because I have been in these places for some time. I had been delivering food to a certain bar that cooks food and has it delivered. I came in early in the day and sometimes late at night. I noticed that the people never left. One day, the woman had to run out to get milk, and I saw her there. They are people who get things delivered but hardly ever go out unless it is a quick trip to the store. If no Christian is ever bold enough to be used to fight for them and go in, how can we get them out?

Further, the women prostitutes have things delivered like McDonald's. They are not allowed to leave. They are forced to work for 12 or more hours straight. After that might be sleep or more partying, the only way you can get to them is to send someone in. My cousin ran a strip bar. I went in to get him out. I was told he wasn't there when I went.

Anyhow, I was talking to the Tipton ministry, which works with the police. The woman who runs it has her husband wait outside in a car. He never goes into the strip club when she goes in there to talk to the ladies. What does she do? She brings another lady in with her to these strip clubs and massage parlors to minister to the women who hardly ever see the light. She gives them food and things. They don't get to eat when they are working, either. She continues to build relationships with them to get them out. Since their ministry started, I have seen a lot of good things. People are getting delivered, shops are going down, and women are getting to see the light of day and even know what day it is again. Did you know when you are having sex with multiple people a day, you are locked in a building? You might not know what day or week it is anymore.

I mentioned the spirit of mammon and sex here. Both are used in witchcraft. Money is used for the control of drugs, witchcraft, and sex. Mammon is usually in the mix to cause poverty and to make rich. Poverty is a spirit, but a lot of poverty people are mixed up with the spirit of mammon.

Delilah was enticed by mammon. She used her manipulation of witchcraft to get Samson. Witchcraft and manipulation go hand in hand. Jezebel, a woman of much witchcraft, is the sister of Delilah though they both lived at different times and had different families. The two were very similar people in the Bible. Remember, Buddha was a person who lived on earth. Jezebel was a person on earth. Delilah was a person on earth. Ahab was a person on earth. You might say, Kathleen, I realize people worship Buddha as god, but these others? Yes. These others. Satan is a prince and has principalities and wicked people who change their names during different centuries. I am not saying that these spirits didn't have names. They did. Satan was Lucifer. There are principalities in the heavens now known as Molech, and so forth. They control money, power, witchcraft, passivity, laziness, and extreme anger. Molech's people on earth are known for having those septum piercings. They have made a pact with this Principality, perhaps unknown to themselves. A spirit enticed them because they agreed with child sacrifice (abortion) and gay and lesbianism. There are real celebrities that have been seduced by unclean spirits that are operating under Molech. The more a person starts to lose modesty and take off their clothes they are seduced and filled with unclean spirits (demons). This is what you see on MTV and television. Our generations are being seduced and brought into sexual perversion by allowing these people on television to tell us this is how we should live. You are watching unclean spirits act out through their bodies. Satan and fallen angel worship is witchcraft. It involves mammon. Can money be used for good? Yes, but what can be used for good, Satan mixes into to use it for bad.

## Incubus and Succubus

There is something I want to acknowledge. Christians suffer greatly in their dream life. I know that the enemy attacks Christians at night. The Lord comes at night to give dreams to Christians and non-Christians. It is no surprise that Satan and demons would attack at night so that the Christian or person might not receive from God. Dreams are often misunderstood. If you don't believe your dreams are from God and you don't know to stop the enemy from being able to work in your life because you didn't break the dream they entered, you might have given the enemy access to your life this way. If you talk about dreams that demons entered and manipulated. They can have a legal right this way. I am not saying you went to someone for help about this and gave the enemy legal access. I am saying if the person doesn't have the discernment to help you spiritually, you can give access to the enemy by talking about the problem so much. The words in our life have power. If you talk about the problem too much, you could make it worse. We have been healed and delivered according to the Word of God. This is what Jesus did for us. This is why I advise not stating the problem so much. I have been plagued in dreams from the enemy. I pray. I destroy Satan's schemes coming into dreams, and it is removed from my memory. I break the things not right in dreams. I paralyze them with the blood of Jesus. I bind the strongman in my dreams or the ones entering them. I paralyze night demons. I stop witches and wizards from coming into my home and entering my dreams while demons are afflicting me at night. I stop them while they work after midnight by stopping altars after midnight and arsenals of Satan. I notice that the enemy might want to vex or come in with his arsenals of strong things at night. They can be destroyed too. He cannot vex us unless we have a curse on us through disobeying God. The enemy of incubus and succubus are sexual demons, male and female. They want to enter people's dream life and do nasty things. Sometimes people get husband spirits and wife spirits attached to them, and they have to be sent out and removed from their dream lives. They can be living in a person. There are spirits that are masturbation and adultery demons too. These want to enter dreams. If we don't know our authority, we can be troubled greatly.

I want you to understand that a person may have gone to the psychiatrist and explained that something entered them in their dreams and had sex with them. The psychiatrist is there to diagnose a disease. This is the only way they can prescribe medicine. The psychiatrist may or may not be a person who understands this and can offer you help through prayer with Jesus. Jesus is the only one who can break this. You are not crazy. These demons are very bad and do these things. The psychiatrist, in order to prescribe medication, has to diagnose schizophrenia. It doesn't mean you have this disease. It means that was the diagnosis because of medical procedures, and this is how they operate. I want to bring this up because people in the community often don't understand spiritual matters and demons. Someone may label you this way when you explain your dreams or the attacks of the enemy. The label is wrong. The situation is spiritual and demonic, and the person needs deliverance. The enemy is wicked, and there are so many generational curses that are on people because of iniquity in the bloodline. The person may have allowed it in through a sexually immoral relationship. God intended man and woman to be in a marriage, and the bed is for the marriage. The bed is not for fornication or for the wrong use of the body in a sexual relationship. If you were ever told by someone you aren't good in bed. This person is probably cheating and wants things a perverse way in bed. The curses come through iniquity. There are people born with mental illnesses that are extreme. They may hit their head against a wall and drool. I know and have worked with individuals like this. They are born with generational curses, and yes, they can be cured.

Also, a person with a curse can manifest hearing voices. They could have come through watching horror movies or through seances. The demons want entry to talk to you and for you to hear from them. The people that are psychics have this manifestation. In society, people label them as schizophrenic. This is the medical disease term for prescribing medication. I want people to stop believing everyone is crazy. If they are lunatics (mentally ill), there is a demon involved. Children can have demon possession, and so can adults. They could have traveled the bloodline. People are not less than you. Don't exalt yourself! They need help. The kingdom of darkness laughs at us because we don't understand the spiritual side of this. Let me explain. I want you to read what a psychiatrist says. The demons often manifest as your husband or wife look alike in your dreams.

If the person doesn't have one, they will take on the characteristic of the people in your life. The people who dream of these things have demons in the house or in their bodies or souls afflicting them. The demons gained access through music, television, games, the internet, or other people you have had sexual encounters with. This is real, and you need deliverance. This is not a joke, and the people below are not crazy. I have permission to discuss their cases. Can a demon gain access through certain drugs? Yes. There are certain demons attached to drugs, especially if you allow addiction to come. Suppose you become addicted to cannabis or some other drug. These demons could have gained access.

## Case 1

"An 18-year-old male, from middle socioeconomic status, who had no family history of any mental illness presented with an insidious onset and continuous illness of 3 years' duration, characterized by the delusion of persecution, the delusion of reference, the delusion of grandiosity, the delusion of control, auditory hallucination of commanding and discussing type, thought broadcast, apathy, poor self-care, and marked socio-occupational dysfunction. In addition to the symptoms listed, he elaborated about someone having sexual intercourse with him against his will. On mental status examination, the patient appeared to be very much distressed with his psychopathology. He described the phenomenon of auditory hallucination (commanding and discussing type) and thought broadcast. In addition, the patient explained that at night, when he would go to his bed, he could feel the sensation of being touched by a female, whom he would describe as a good-looking woman. He would be able to feel his private parts being touched, leading to erection and ejaculation. As per the patient, he did not want this experience; this would happen against his will, he would feel guilty about having such an experience and having sexual contact with an unknown female, and he was fully convinced about having such an experience. Very occasionally, he would get up from sleep after this experience and remain distressed and fearful. In his explanation, he had a strong belief that a "witch" was doing so but would not be able to point out the exact figure of the "witch." His cognitive functions were intact, and he had poor insight.

There was no history suggestive of narcolepsy, insomnia, hypersomnia, sleep terrors, nightmares, sleep-related movement disorders, and sleep paralysis; symptoms suggestive of Dhat syndrome, panic attacks, posttraumatic stress disorder, cognitive deficits, and recent change in medications. Based on the available information, a diagnosis of schizophrenia was considered. His investigations in the form of a hemogram, renal function test, liver function test, serum electrolytes, thyroid function test, electroencephalogram, and magnetic resonance imaging of the brain did not reveal any abnormality. He was started on aripiprazole which was increased up to 15 mg/day, with which all his symptoms, including the phenomenon of succubus, improved completely. He would now report a lack of any such experience but was not sure about the previous experience being real or part of the illness.

## Case 2

A 24-year-old male who has been using cannabis in a dependent pattern presented with an insidious onset and continuous illness of 2 years' duration, characterized by the delusion of reference, delusional percept, the delusion of love, auditory (commenting, commanding, and discussing), and tactile hallucinations. At presentation, on mental status examination, he was untidy and ill-kempt and had blunt affect; however, there was no formal thought disorder. When asked about his psychopathology, he ascribed the voices heard to one of his female teachers, who would express her love toward him in the conversations heard as part of the auditory hallucinations. He also ascribed the tactile hallucinations to the same teacher. He described this as a sensation of vibration, which he would feel all over his body, more so in his thighs and genital region. This would occur mainly at night when he would be fully awake or asleep and alone, would feel aroused, and simultaneously hear the voice of his teacher claiming to be responsible for these sensations. As per him, he would hear that she is in deep love with him and wanted to have sexual intercourse with him, would feel his penis to be touched, and in the process, would have an erection and occasional ejaculation. He would be unable to describe exactly how she would be doing this but was convinced that it was she who was doing so. He also believed that his body was under the control of his teacher, who forced him to indulge in sexual activities against his will. He would deny drawing any pleasure out of these activities and would say that he was not able to avoid this experience. This experience was not associated with any active cannabis use or abstinence from cannabis. At the time of the mental status examination, his cognitive functions were preserved, and he had poor insight.

Due to all these symptoms, he had to discontinue his education and became homebound. Based on the available information, a diagnosis of schizophrenia and cannabis dependence syndrome was considered, and he was sequentially treated with olanzapine, risperidone, Trifluoperazine, and the combination of olanzapine and fluphenazine decanoate, in adequate doses for adequate duration. He showed 40%–50% improvement in auditory hallucinations but no significant change in tactile hallucinations with these medications. Finally, he responded to clozapine at the dose of 200 mg/day. After being treated with clozapine, his insight improved; he would acknowledge that all his previous symptoms were unreal and part of the illness."[1]

# Chapter 11 - Witchcraft that Brought Poverty

I see this a lot in some towns. I have one city where there are several driving all hours of the day without a license plate. This tells you the spirit of rebellion is in your town like wildfire.

You have a poverty spirit stronghold in this neighborhood that
needs to be taken down.

You have a poverty spirit and Ahab spirit in this neighborhood.

**This is a resemblance to a place where the renters are here for a cheaper stay. I was approached by a couple of pimps outside the door of a prostitute when I was at a place like this. I delivered slushes to a place like this. Outside in a vehicle, two pimps. They tried to talk to me. I got in my car and left quickly. At this particular place, I had a drunk man trying to get me to stay when I delivered food.**

In the first picture, I show that someone is driving around without a license plate. I mentioned that in one city, there are people at all hours of the day driving around without a license plate. I asked someone in the community about it. I was told the police don't care too much about it. It is not a priority for them. They hardly pull anyone over for it. Well, if the police don't care about rebellion against the law, why should the people care? This particular city has so much witchcraft done in it. The problem of rebellion has gone on for years. There are multiple sex shops, legal prostitution places, clubs, extreme poverty, corrupt politics, abortion clinic, liquor stores, smoke shops, and more. The Bible says, *"And Samuel said, Hath the LORD as great delight in burnt offerings and sacrifices, as in obeying the voice of the LORD? Behold, to obey is better than sacrifice, and to hearken than the fat of rams. For rebellion is as the sin of witchcraft, and stubbornness is as iniquity and idolatry. Because thou hast rejected the word of the LORD, he hath also rejected thee from being king."* 1 Samuel 15:22-23. There are people of God in this community that has become corrupted. They vote for abortion. Now I understand the people in the community are extremely gay and lesbian. What happened? Witchcraft. This is a well-known city. The children in the city are extremely rebellious. Again, the witchcraft communities pray in these principalities each year to cover these territories. This is what you see on the ground. It was prayed in by witchcraft. The principality brought in alcoholism one year, drugs the next, poverty the next, and so on. These are principalities. Let's look at the next principality.

**This is a strip run by drugs, sex, money, and prostitution. I want to expound on this more in writing.**

I am pointing this out to you to know what you are up against. You
now have allowed several principalities to take over this town. This
has gone on for years and years. The principality you have this
year still has last year in operation because of the people who
didn't tear it down and who operate with God's authority.

This Motel advertises that it has the god of money, alcohol, and sex operating it. You can get adult movies, liquor, novelties (sex toys), and lotto (god of mammon), and there is a vacancy. Why? This is rented by the hour, possibly. This is along a strip with several motels and hotels in a row. There is a pimp here, I am sure.

Why did I mention Homeless Programs here? I mentioned it for a reason. I want to point out that in some towns, the Homeless get into a program. The program is that they are dropped off at various locations around the city. The motel people tell them they will pick them up in 10 hours. They collect as much money as they can from the people that pass by them all day on the road. If you see a lot of homeless people in the town, you have the principality that brought in a vagabond spirit. Now, homeless people are to be loved. I don't want you to think you must pass by and not help them. This is wrong. We are commanded to love them and show them the love of God. This includes helping them with food, money, work, and the help they need to get out of the situations they are enslaved in or have fallen into. They are no less than any other person on this earth. I love them. I talk to them. I check on them. I speak to them about my troubles and ask them about theirs. This is a living person who could be any of us if we lose our home and spouse, and money source. If the Motel is helping them, perhaps, this is more than we are. If they are addicted or something worse, this is still a person who we must treat with love.

The police aren't the only ones on the ground here. We, as Christians, are on the ground too. We have to help the officers. They see firsthand what the principality has brought in through the ground demons. These ground demons cannot operate unless they have received the instructions from the principality above. That's where we come in. We have authority from heaven. We take our authority from Jesus, who is seated in the highest heaven. Did you know that? Your authority is from the highest heaven. This means you operate in authority over the second heaven, and eventually, you are to operate over the moon, stars, planets, meteor showers, and the things on earth, like the waters of the sea, storms, and animals. You also exercise your authority over witches and wizards trying to kill, steal and destroy you. You are over the authority of Satan and demons. Therefore, exercise your authority and pray with spiritual warfare praying. This way, you stop evil. This way, you prevent evil. This way, you operate with what was given to you by the LORD.

# Chapter 12 - Children Being Killed in Schools

Things are first natural then spiritual. But the things you see on the ground have something going on in the unseen realm. There are principalities in the second heaven. Satan is on the ground and up there. The territorial demons that walk the ground are taking orders from them up there and even from hell. You see that the astral projection is done at night when the person sleeps. The demon takes them out of their body and does things on the ground and in the heavens to take out people. The church must fight this off. The Bible teaches that some things can only be done by prayer and fasting. The Bible teaches that the people of God fast when an enemy comes in and does this kind of thing. There must be something going on in that community in the individual homes with a falling away for it even to be allowed to happen. The Lord protects us, but when we allow our lives to be given over to Satan and demons, the Lord chastens us. A judgment can only come when the enemy has gone up to heaven and argued in the court that he has legal rights unless the Lord permits it as he did in Job to show forth the righteousness of his saints. But I truly believe that this is not the case in the shootings going on in the schools. I heard a preacher named David Taylor state that the Lord showed him that Satan does not argue as you think he would up there. You might think he argues that there is sexual immorality or adultery, or some other sin. He argues that the people have no fruit. The people are not loving, full of joy, peaceful, patient, kind, gentle, good, faithful, or even merciful. The Lord permits the enemy to attack because he has won the argument against his saints. In order to stop these attacks in the schools and wherever they are manifesting, this is what you need to know and do.

"These are demonic forces that are being transferred from one region to another. These are patterns and cycles of the devil. How we combat this in the spirit realm as believers is, as soon as we see something like this manifest, we dismantle it through prayer and fasting in the spirit realm so it will not carry over to other locations that will affect our generation. We need to curse it, cut it, and uproot it-and that's how we accomplish through Christ Jesus and the Holy Spirit to defeat the enemy and his game plan."[2]

I am for raising assault weapon age requirements. I think that it is a lethal deadly weapon. I do want my second amendment rights. What happens if a country comes in, and we can't fight because all our guns are taken away? I recall that weapons taken away does happen. Do you remember in the Bible, Saul and Jonathan had weapons, but the Israelites didn't? How could another country come in and take away all the weapons for them to fight with? I believe we need laws. Be careful what you allow the enemy to take away because if he can work to strip you down, he will. This way, you will not be able to fight a bigger army. You will have to know how to fight in the spirit when this comes. What happens when the LORD's judgment is severe?

## Altars in the Heavenlies

Did you know that you are to set up altars and put them up to the throne room of God? You can use the one at the church and pray. You can bend your knees anywhere and pray.

But know that the enemy has demonic altars and satanic altars too. These are set up to create patterns and cycles. The altars need to be brought down, and the patterns and cycles of repeat. What is a pattern and cycle? It can be many things. I heard Pastor Ray of Faith Christian Assembly talking about this. He was preaching that he knows of many people that get out of a situation because the Lord delivered them. But they go right back into it. I truly believe that the person has not demolished the altars and patterns of the cycle of repeat in the spiritual realm. But know that it might have been demolished, and the person didn't understand that once they were delivered, they had to go and build up those places that the Lord just delivered them from. Let me show you. I drank when I was married at some point, on a lot of occasions. I remember getting out of the marriage and when I was living on my own in another state at the beginning of 2011. I had a pattern of drinking setup, so when I got home to an empty apartment on Friday night. I didn't know what to do. So, I went out and bought beer. I was going to a Christian church. I listened to secular radio. I had never liked Christian stations. Well, I opened the 12th beer to drink it. I was not content with the radio music. I turned the station to a Christian station and found contentment. When I woke up the next morning, I came to and realized God had probably saved my life again. This was it. I stopped drinking. That was over ten years ago. I had a pattern with the Lord that was righteous too. I read my Bible every day and all the way through every year. Because of this godly pattern, when the enemy came knocking through people and temptations, I could say, no way. My LORD loves me enough, and I have overcome. I am not going there anymore. I love the Holy Spirit more than that buzz. I fight with the Lord's stronghold, not my own strength. The enemy will bring people in to get you back into that lifestyle of bars and drinking. I have had family weddings where I was asked several times to drink and family Christmas parties and so forth. I say no. Why? I want the Lord not that high. I have people come and ask to live with me. I have people come and ask me out on dates. I have lots of temptations. But I build my life up in the Lord so that I know how to discern who and of what fruit they are that is talking to me. You might say, I am cute, But I know what fruit is talking to me. Come on! I have a prayer life. I am in community. I read my Bible. I study. I listen to sermons and apply principles. If you apply principles, you can defeat his attacks. I want the Lord's help, and if it is overwhelming and it gets there, I rely on his strength, not my own. This is how you fight. You learn spiritual warfare. You can win the battle in the spiritual realm and tear down the enemy territories. I hear Satanists laugh at us because we don't know how to fight as Christians. They know more about the spiritual realm than us. This should not be. You have to learn, and you have to fight. The police officer and military need your help. They see what is on the ground. But you have to fight like them. You have to fight it off in the spiritual realm to help them win on the ground. You have to do it. The military is fighting, and the police are fighting. But what are you doing? You have to fight. You are enlisted as a warfighter the day you accept Christ (Rev. 12:17). Fight. You can either not fight and be defeated, or you can fight and be a warrior. You can fight and be an elite warrior enlisted as a special force fighter who has much experience. Get the experience. Get the knowledge and understanding too. Then, use it as wisdom on the ground and in the air, and in the second heaven. Fight, soldier, fight. There is a place for you in the kingdom of God to be a King and for some emperors.

*"See, I have this day set thee over nations, and over kingdoms, to root out, and to pull down, and to destroy, and to throw down, to build and to plant. And I will utter my judgments against them touching all their wickedness, who have forsaken me, and have burned incense unto other gods, and worshipped the works of their hands. Thou, therefore, gird up thy loins and arise, and speak unto them all that I command thee: be not dismayed at their faces, lest I confound thee before them. For, behold, I have made thee this day a defenced city, and an iron pillar, and a brazen wall against the whole land, against the kings of Judah, against the princes thereof, against the priests thereof, and*

*against the people of the land. And they shall fight against thee, but they shall not prevail against thee; for I am with thee, saith the LORD, to deliver thee."* Jeremiah 1:10, 16-19.

# Pray

*I pray over the nations, Lord, and over the Kingdoms. I call on the name of Jesus, whom I serve and am seated with. I pull down all demonic altars that are set up against my children, ministry, and me. I level them to nothing. I demobilize and disable all demons that are put to guard me in my times and seasons. I throw down all chanting and hindering with blocking that was brought forth to stop me. I destroy by charge the assaults of the enemy and shell them until they are no more. They are no more in Jesus name. I bind all demonic persons who are astral projecting into my house and neighborhood. I root out by cursing the job duty and function of the enemy and his workers that are trying to kill, steal and destroy from me. I proclaim that you will fall down in the holes you have dug up for me. I proclaim you will be put into the place you wanted for me and my own. I will have everything Father has for me. The Word of the Lord says that our God is a consuming fire. Therefore, I declare Holy Spirit to attack you with fire and get you off of my body now. I am cleansed, sanctified, healed, and delivered. I throw down and curse all Satanic altars and the things the workers of the Satanic world have put on them to represent me and my ministry. I am defeating you now with the blood of Jesus. I am aware that the Lord said, "That which the palmerworm hath left the locust eaten; and that which the locust hath left the cankerworm eaten; and that which the cankerworm hath left the caterpillar eaten. The Lord said in Joel this, and I know why you are here. But he also said I will restore to you the years that were lost to this great army of Satan. I send the blood of Jesus out now to destroy demons, fallen angels, and Satan. I am a watchman on the wall, and I will not allow you to come and take me or my church and family down any longer. God when the enemy comes up a level to destroy me, because I moved up a level. I defeat him by my testimony. My Lord Jesus took me out of your hands and said she is now a New Creation. I defeat him by the blood of the lamb. The blood has defeated you and stripped you of all your authority against me. I know you constantly set up altars against me in the spirit realm. Your square and compass, pentagrams, and rolling stones are done. You are defeated. I pull them down and use them for fire. I take your banners. The strategy you have against me,*

# Astral Projection

How does someone astral project? Did you know the Lord talks about this in the Bible? The enemy, I have heard, once you are his and have died, has the right to grab you out of the body and take you to hell. The demon would take you down to hell and show you where your forever home will be. What does the Bible say about this?

*"Or ever the silver cord be loosed, or the golden bowl be broken, or the pitcher be broken at the fountain, or the wheel broken at the cistern." Ecclesiastes 12:6*

The silver cord is what is used by the enemy to pull the person out of the body to go and do his work. If the silver cord is broken, the person will die. Sometimes the Lord sends the person back into the body through the silver cord if there is a watchman up at seasons and nights at the time they come. The person is equipped to know when they are coming and what to do. This is the praying I tell you about knowing about their times and the moon cycles. The person is always at significant risk when the enemy and demons pull them out of their body to lose their life. But the enemy will use them anyways. The person that astral projects can do this a thousand times because the Lord has allowed them time to repent. They can feel skilled at witchcraft and doing this to put you and me as Christians in a dismantling position. This happens and continues. Rise up. Let's kick them out of our lives and our schools and towns.

"As a demonic priest, at night, I would leave my body and fly over neighborhoods, hurling taunts and curses down on the people who lived within their borders. Caught in the grip of strange dreams, I would feel myself being transported into different neighborhoods within the five boroughs of New York City. These out-of-body experiences (called astral projection) allowed me to have dominion over the communities. I felt diabolical, like a vampire, and I knew they had nothing on me. Sometimes I would even land and walk around the neighborhoods, bringing curses, bad luck, and a witchcraft aura. Oddly, however, in some neighborhoods, I met with strong resistance and, at first, couldn't understand where the opposing power came from. In these neighborhoods, people were waiting for me to land; I prepared to curse the neighborhood, but when I landed, a mob would chase me for blocks, and I couldn't curse them. Frustrated, I would fly off again, hovering as high as the streetlamps, and they would look up at me. Finally, I realized these were nasty Christians praying for their neighborhoods, their communities, and their families-the prayers of the people I hated the most. Wherever these praying Christians lived, I couldn't penetrate the neighborhood. I got in, but I couldn't do the evil acts I had come to perform. So, I would move on to the next neighborhood."[2]

# Pray

*Lord, the occultists, Satanists, warlocks, witches, and the people that are devoted to Satan are astral projecting into my church building and my home and the home of my family, who are the believers. It now comes to my knowledge that those noises I hear in my home of someone walking around and opening doors and even picking up my things are a worker of darkness sent by Satan to see what I am doing and to find a pattern in my life to create patterns and cycles over me to destroy my life and my calling and my destiny. The word of the Lord says what I bind is bound on earth. I bind these witches and warlocks now. I destroy their silver cord. I ask that you afflict them until they repent. I close all demonic doors they are using for astral projection now. I send seven arrows of fire into the enemy's camp and defeat Satan and demons now. The enemy has targeted the church. So, I target the enemy now. I target him and take him out right now with the blood of the LAMB, Jesus our Messiah. Jesus our Yeshua. You defeated the works of the enemy, and You called us to do this through You. I understand that there are groupings of angels in heaven. Gabriel is over Seraphim and Cherubim under Megatron. Then, Michael, who is over human virtue and the nations, and Raphael, who is over the spirits of men. Uriel, who is over clamor and terror; Raguel, who inflicts punishment on the world and the luminaries; and Sarakiel, who is over spirits of children that transgress. The book of Enoch mentions these and the others over the things of heaven and on the elements there and those upon the earth. The church has been afflicted, and I want the church to know that the angels are fighting for you now. I understand very great evil is being done to the body of Christ from all sides. So, from every side, I send the Holy Ghost consuming fire against you Satanists and occultists. The Bible talks about schemes and wiles. I take that to heart, and I now destroy your schemes and wiles demons and the witches and the high priests now against the church. Where you used a blood sacrifice to bring upon your chanting to cast down our leaders and people of God, I destroy it now. I take out your altars now. I know that when we have the darkness come over the earth as God promised. The darkness that comes over that God said would be a sign to us, and it is. Lord, the witches use what your church doesn't understand to put on a heaviness that cannot be broken unless the church grows in understanding that the solar eclipse is used by these people to put things into the spirit realm and planting to take what you have for the Christians. I pray that the body rises up at these times and prays and fasts to destroy it before it takes root. Let those that have rooted bad over your people be destroyed. The graveyard work the enemy uses, and the deep voodoo and hoodoo are now destroyed. I destroy the workings that are leading your people astray by entertaining talking to dead relatives now. Necromancy is being propagated on the screen today in heaviness, and your people are watching it and entertaining the kingdom of darkness wiles. I destroy this in the spirit. Lord, send angels of their responsibility now to take down witchcraft in my area here where I live in this place and this territory of the principality. I release blindness into the enemy's camp to destroy them coming into your church and releasing the horrible wizardry and sorceries on your people. The book of Exodus did talk about how easy it was for these people to do magic. Let it be a lesson. It is still that easy, and the body needs to wake up. This is done in secret and is taking our people out. I declare their works are now done away with. We send the blood of Jesus to destroy your workings now. I will send confusion into the witches and wizards and high priests' camp now. You will repent. Lord, I see that the growth of the church stops when sin comes in. Then, the camp of demons comes in with astral projectors and puts up the cycles that stop the growth. The church gets stuck in a pit and needs to be pulled out. I destroy the cycles and now ask for angel assistance to help the people and leaders out. Lord, you said at Babel that you confused languages. So, frustrate their communications now, let their words seem dumb and not be understood, and let the witchcraft places where they meet be pulled down and plucked up now. I destroy them in Jesus' name. I curse them in Jesus' name. You are finished here in my church and here in my region. Father, I shut down the first and second heavens and now say that the Satanists and occultists are shut down with it. I shut down so that the principalities could not give their orders to the demons on the ground, in our Lord, and Savior, and Redeemer, and Deliverer, and Conquerors name, Jesus Christ. Oh, Everlasting Father of all times and seasons and days and years and all there is and always will be, Amen.*

# Chapter 13 - Spiritualism

What is spiritualism? It is focused on good deeds, not faith in Jesus Christ. I have found that at the church of Satan, it comes in many forms to appeal to people. Again, it is called many things in your neighborhoods. I have found multiple names, including Bahai Church or Retreat, Bahais Church, Metaphysical Church, New Age Church, Spiritualist Church, etc. The church will address the public that the members are from many religions. This will entice you to come. The church wants you to know that Buddhists, Christians, and many others are part of the people who attend. Are they lying? No. They are telling you the truth. It is their job to evangelize to bring over people from other religions to the church of Satan. They really focus on Christians.

Christians are attacked by witchcraft by the people at these churches. The reason is there is warfare going on. Christians stand against this church and stop in the spirit realm what the church of Satan is trying to do. They are working for Satan and demon spirits that these people believe guide them in the spirit world in order to help their god in the world accomplish his goals. The people who are Christians are praying against the workings of their god, named Satan. They have one god. They believe in one god. Their god is the highest being. The funniest thing is that the church of Satan proclaims it believes in ONE GOD, although they worship many gods.

The spiritualist believes very much in the spirit world. They are the ones that are drawn out of their body through astral projection and identify that the spirit is real. They believe that everyone lives in the spirit world after they die. But the spirit world has nice places for good people and bad places for bad people. If a bad person wants to go to a better place, the person will have to do good in the spirit world. They don't gravitate to a hell place. They believe in lies. The spiritualist believes they are kept in spirit form in the spirit world and can do good to improve. Thus, the spirit person, after death, can communicate with living beings on earth to help them too.

# Psychics

**The Witch of En-dor**

*"Then said Saul unto his servants, Seek me a woman that hath a familiar spirit, that I may go to her, and enquire of her. And his servants said to him, Behold, there is a woman that hath a familiar spirit at En-dor. And Saul disguised himself, and put on other raiment, and he went, and two men with him, and they came to the woman by night: and he said, I pray thee, divine unto me by the familiar spirit, and bring me him up, whom I shall name unto thee. And the woman said unto him, Behold, thou knowest what Saul hath done, how he hath cut off those that have familiar spirits, and the wizards, out of the land: wherefore then layest thou a snare for my life, to cause me to die? And Saul sware to her by the LORD, saying, As the LORD liveth, there shall no*

*punishment happen to thee for this thing. Then said the woman, Whom shall I bring up unto thee? And he said, Bring me up Samuel. And when the woman saw Samuel, she cried with a loud voice: and the woman spake to Saul, saying, Why hast thou deceived me? For thou art Saul. And the king said to her, Be not afraid: for what sawest thou? And the woman said unto Saul, I saw gods ascending out of the earth. And he said unto her, What form is he of? And she said, An old man cometh he is covered in a mantle. And Saul perceived that it was Samuel, and he stooped with his face to the ground, and bowed himself. And Samuel said to Saul, Why hast thou disquieted me, to bring me up? And Saul answered, I am sore distressed; for the Philistines make war against me, and God is departed from me, and answereth me no more, neither by prophets, nor by dreams: therefore, I have called thee, that thou mayest make known unto me what I shall do. Then said Samuel, Wherefore then dost thou ask of me, seeing the LORD is departed from thee, and is become thine enemy? And the LORD hath done to him, as he spake by me: for the LORD hath rent the kingdom out of thine hand, and given to thy neighbor, even to David: because thou obeyest not the voice of the LORD, nor executedst his fierce wrath upon Amalek, therefore hath the LORD done this thing unto thee this day. Moreover, the LORD will also deliver Israel with thee into the hand of the Philistines: and tomorrow shalt thou and thy sons be with me: the LORD also shall deliver the host of Israel into the hand of the Philistines.* " 1 Samuel 28:7-19

This passage is confusing because Samuel talked with Saul. The Catholics believe you can communicate with the dead. Catholics believe that on some occasions, a person in purgatory can communicate with you in a limited words way. They believe you can pray for intercession from the dead. The spiritualists communicate with the dead. The people who do witchcraft communicate with the dead. The passage is about Saul communicating with the dead. The woman saw gods. She said she saw gods. What form of gods did she see? Usually, when this happens, a person who has a familiar spirit sees a demon acting on behalf of the dead. The demons are great at mimicking a person's identity and characteristics. They do this to fool you. I know firsthand. It has been done to me. They mimic someone that has passed away to the tee. They act and talk and can even look just like them. The principalities that rule in the heavens have taken on the past identity of a person. The demons on the ground do the same thing. When I was fifteen, my neighbors took me and did a séance so I could communicate with my mother who passed away. I wasn't afraid. I thought she was really communicating with me. The neighbors took me aside beforehand and wanted to console me with the loss of my mother. They said we can help you get in touch with your mother. I had never heard of such a thing, and I said yes. I was in so deep of sadness as a young woman in the 10th grade. I wanted to talk to her again. The person communicating with me said they were my mother and answered the questions I asked. Then, after this experience my neighbors wouldn't let me go home to my dad. They said I had to stay the night. A woman present insisted I sleep next to her that night to not be afraid. I wasn't afraid, but some force that was evil attacked me that night and made me afraid. The king, Saul, has now made an agreement with a woman who communicates with Satan and demons. Satan now has the upper hand. The king ended up losing the war and his life and his son's lives. He went to the enemy and asked for help. He should not have gone to a witch. What really happened? Bo Ra Choi explained there were two spirits present. One in the woman and one outside the woman making all this happen. Apostle, David E. Taylor, explained that the witch really did talk to Samuel, because at this time the saint was in hell, Sheol, and she could communicate with him. The Bible attests to saints being in hell until Jesus brought them up from Sheol. Apostle Taylor said that Samuel actually prophesied the death of Saul.

What happened here with the witch? She might have believed her life's hopes had returned. She could practice again and even get the king on her side. The woman had the demonic realm stolen from her mind. The spiritualist believes that they have mental abilities as a medium called clairvoyance, where they see spirits and clairaudience, where they hear voices of Satan, fallen angels, and demons, and clairsentience, where they have senses exercised to be able to sense a spirit in the room. The truth is that the person needs deliverance because the demons were after their mind to control it and have succeeded. The person who is a medium also has medium physical abilities of the demonic. They have demons speak through them and can find their bodies lifting in levitation. If you are a Christian and are still experiencing these things even after Holy Spirit Baptism, seek renunciation and deliverance. You will most likely need help with this. You must fast and pray. But you need help from a deliverance minister or another Christian to get them off of you. They are not in your spirit but may be attached to your soul and body. The church of Satan often emanates this to the people to speak to them. The person has a demon inside of them who is talking to the people and having a great time with you. The medium will have a demon appear and tell them things. The demon will tell them with accuracy what happened in the past and now is going on and show them the patterns and cycles to tell them what is coming to the earth. It is a twisted view of Satan. This way, the demons plan to kill more of mankind in a bigger way. Please be aware. Demons and Satan speak through many people's voices. You don't have to be a psychic. You just have to be a human being they can mess with.

# Chapter 14 - Spirits in Religion

**This is a picture of Santeria worship. It is supposed to be Michael the archangel. Tear it down in your community. The witches meet here to take you down. They are not your friends in this restaurant. Love them. Speak kindly to them but take down the meeting place of Santeria here. The Lord will ensure that it stops. The people still can make food for the community, but the witchcraft needs to be cursed to the root here.**

The scary thing about mediums in the church is that they are manipulating the church to seek after the dead for help. They have done it in the Catholic church in a big way. The Catholic church celebrates feasts for the dead and prays to them. I don't necessarily believe celebrating a Feast in remembrance of someone in the past is wrong. This is admirable that the Catholic church remembers the past heroes.

But in the Catholic church, the congregation prays for the dead that their soul might leave purgatory and go to heaven. Also, Catholics pray to people they believe are in heaven, like past Saints. The idea of a soul in purgatory comes from Maccabees. In II Maccabees 12:39-45 the Script is taken out of context. The real way it should be read is Judas realized that his fellow Jews had died because they were idol worshippers. If you go back a little, it tells you that Judas called upon the Lord and sang Psalms with a loud voice to stop his men from getting killed. God heard his cry and helped the Jews. Then, God showed Judas why they were dying. The men were idol worshippers, and this brought destruction to the Jews. Well, Judas and his men were happy God showed them why these men died, and they besought the Lord not to remember this sin against Israel in the future. Then, the words tell us that there will be a resurrection in the future. One to be judged in righteousness and the other in his sins. The hope of Judas was the resurrection of the godly. He made a reconciliation for the living Jews so that God would remember them in the future as godly men. This clearly is asking God not to judge Israel for the sins that were committed by these men. This is not the Script telling us that people go to a place called purgatory and to pray for them there to be able to go to heaven. As for worshipping in the Catholic church, the worshipper that bows down to Mary, Michael, or any other saint is called an idol worshipper. We are not to make graven images and bow down to them. There are examples of angels telling humans not to bow down to them. There is an example of Saint Paul telling people not to bow down to him.

It is similar to the church of Satan and Santeria. They celebrate Feasts and Saints and worship the dead. Their Feasts are not like Catholic Feasts. In October alone, the church of Satan celebrates at least 7 Feasts. You are giving your legal rights over and being manipulated by demons. Here in this picture of Santeria, you have an image called Michael, where the Catholic church has venerated what they say was an apparition of Michael in the 400s. They say he is a saint. I understand a saint is someone that has been given life through Jesus Christ and has received the forgiveness of sins. Michael is an archangel. What if this apparition was not really Michael? The oldest apparition was with Adam and Eve. Satan appeared to Adam and Eve in a different form. Apparitions are of the enemy. I see the worship of Michael as a Saint in the Catholic church and in Santeria. Santeria worships saints. They are also experts in spiritualism and witchcraft. They communicate with angels who fell from heaven and who could pretend to be Michael.

## Regla Lucumi, Regla de Ocha, Santería

The same in all three. It is the worship of Saints and, ultimately worship of many gods.

There is a Taqueria in this gas station. The taqueria, along with serving food and drink, has Santeria worship in it. There is an idol on display with an offering. The witchcraft is taking place at this store, along with the gas station selling you other demonic items. This is a serious stronghold in your town.

This is a place you bring children for a treat after school. But it is also a place where Santeria witchcraft is done. You might think you are treating your kids to afterschool treats, but you are exposing your children to Santeria. The people that run this place are equipped to enter your home during astral projection and change your life for the negative by obeying the demons to know how to take your family down. See the next picture.

The god on the Pepsi cooler is worshipped by giving it flowers. It is a Santeria place. The church of Satan owns this place. It is not a place to hang out. There are real people in here that need Jesus. But know what you are entering when going in there. They are the ones Satan is using to take your family down at night.

235

Santeria or Regla Lucumi or Regla de Ochan is commonly referred to as worshipping the way of the saints. You will end up understanding that you are truly worshipping fallen angels and Satan, whom these people understand to be deities. You will find that this religion has combined the use of voodoo in Yoruba and Roman Catholic worship of Christianity to worship the dead and saints, along with worshipping many demons. There are centralized deities in this religion called oricha. These are the principalities in the heavens. They are one and the same as Allah in Islam and so forth. I understand in Santeria you know the name to be different, but it is the same fallen angel that you might know liking green the best and over Africa. It is for the people to communicate with the principality that they are assigned to, who is called a deity. The people believe that they are touching the creator, who manifests as Olodumare. They are using his force, as believed, called aché to be able to control things and move them to their desires or the god's desire. The demonic rituals cause these things to happen. The demons use the manipulation of people and astral projection to make things happen in the night and change the life of the communities to further the kingdom of Satan. I have shown you the pictures above to let you know they are giving these gods offerings of flowers. There are other offerings required, including animals.

The people who follow this religion believe there is one central god whom they refer to as three in view. God is not three persons, but there are three ways he is seen. Oldumare is the name of the creator. He is also called Olofi and Olorun. Olodumare made all that there is. Olofi lives in all of the created beings and things. Olorun is the god who created all animals and humans and oricha and angels. The people do not generally give any gifts to Olodumare. They give gifts, flowers, animal sacrifices, and so forth to the oricha. See, they give their offerings to saints and to the deities (fallen angels). They believe this makes the creator happy to give his saints and fallen angels worship. The saints they venerate like Catholics.

The oricha are deities to the Santerians. The Santerians communicate with these deities who operate in the second heaven. They are usually working with one deity, as they believe in their lives whom they were suited to be in contact with and assigned to their lives. As seen above, the people giving flowers to the god (deity) in the pictures, it is believed that certain people have become a deity who once lived. Santerians believe that a deity was created by their god before the humans or that the deity became a god after they lived. Some gods who are the deities to them are Lazarus, who was once a human. They call him Babalu Ave.

In Santeria and witchcraft circles, mediums exist. These mediums believe that Jesus guides them. Jesus to them was a medium, and when they started to receive visions of him, they understood he was their guide in the spirit world. The reality of what they see, as I understand very well and can share with great confidence, is a false vision. It is divination. Divination is what the enemy brings to show you false visions. They can see the truth too. If they are going to fight, an army of God called Christians and Israelites. They can see that they will not succeed. In this circle, the mediums use herbs and oils and good foods and drinks. Just like our Christian God tells us to take care of our bodies, Satan stole from heaven. He tells them to take care of their body.

Anyhow, the mediums are the people who are treating people as a doctor. However, they might not be licensed in that sense. They have gone to many classes to help people be healed by Satan. Satan and his crew can put forth false healing. They simply stop hurting you for a time to show you that you have been healed. However, it is not so. You will just turn around at another time to be hurt again. This is their false healing. I have seen it in my own body. The demons have legal rights. They stop hurting me for a season. Looks like I am healed. But there was a generational curse in the bloodline or something I opened up myself to in life that allowed them to have access. We as a church must step up and enforce spiritual warfare training in the church, or it is going to continue downhill in our churches.

In the Roman Catholic church, there are many involved in Santeria witchcraft. The church had collided with Cuba and West Africa's witchcraft through communicating with the dead. Thus, the three are often mixed in Santeria's worship of the saints. There are some in Santeria that want to kick out Catholic forms of worship. I believe it is because Catholics believe in the triune God, the one and only true God. This angers the witchcraft community because you are warring against what they are trying to do. The people refer to themselves as practitioners who are called mediums. They are the ones who have brought healing through the use of divination/chakras. One of the oricha's (principalities, fallen angels), named, Yemaja, is known to ask the people in this religion to dress in white for a long season. Other parts of Santeria or other religions mixed in are Palo. Palo is the darker side. Palo uses skulls, roots, and bones to bring a spiritual entity inside the home. They use things for the result of healing themselves and for protection from bad spirits. So, they may use a spirit to hurt you moreover. In the time of Nimrod, Terah was the leader of the hosts of the war. In Terah's home, there were gods made. Then, in Rachel and Leah's home growing up, their dad had entities to communicate with. Rachel stole gods from her father. Some entities were made in communities through a part of the head of a firstborn son. The entity would talk through the head to communicate things of truth. I said it. The entity told them truths, but it was for their purpose to destroy the family.

While Santeria is said to use light to help them be more successful and live good lives, a lot of witchcraft churches practice Santeria, Palo Mayombe, and other forms of religion. They communicate with dead relatives and the oricha with divination. They use divination to determine what kind of sacrifice the oricha tells them is needed, like a chicken or human. These sacrifices, in turn, give the person more power from Satan, fallen angels, and the demons. The person often is to eat the organs. These people are known to have human bones either that they bought or that they have participated in a cultic kill. Where are the people missing going? Have you ever wondered where a child goes? The children taken are among some they sacrifice. I believe that some are sold to families, others sold abroad, some I don't know, and some are used for killings to be sacrificed. I know today that the witchcraft people do not go to the doctor to tell them they are pregnant and then give the child up for sacrifice. We have no record then that a woman was pregnant. Children are killed because they are thought to be innocent. Therefore, they are the perfect sacrifice to their deities (fallen angels). Yes, they are killing children to sacrifice to a fallen angel that is destined for the lake of fire. Yes, they are enticed to kill innocent souls just so they can be forgiven and live good lives on this earth and in the spirit world. This is the falsehood these people are held by in these witchcraft churches. Stop playing nice with these people and letting them tell their stories in the local paper. Stop posting where their church is and that there is a psychic fair there. Stop this. You are hurting innocent lives. I don't care if they paid the fee to post in the paper. Tell them no. Curse these places and uproot them from the community before your children are hurt. The word says to exercise Christ's authority. Suppose you don't know how to go by these places in your community and uproot them. I am telling you how. Take them by the throat and curse them by standing in front of the building and taking hold of it and praying against it and telling it to fall and telling it you will hurt here no more. You are finished.

In Bakersfield, California, in the 80s, children came forth and stated to the police that they were forced to participate in Satanic rituals of killings and cannibalism. This was posted in the paper. When they offer up their babies, they drink the blood and eat the heart. In America, many people go missing. They are taken from us for purposes of killing and for human prostitution. In Santeria, many have allegiance to various types of religions and their practices. But it is noted that the priests and priestesses want people to acknowledge they are Roman Catholic. It is probably a deception of sorts on the person who thinks that it is better to convert someone who acknowledges Jesus as Lord over to their witchcraft religion. There are other people who join Santeria that believe they are Jews and are considered Hindu or Buddhist and so forth.

Santeria practitioners believe they are true believers. Further, those that participate in the religion of witchcraft in Santeria are called children of oricha. Thus, they even call themselves the children of fallen angels. The Bible says they are children of the devil. Thus, they prove themselves to be by their own names. *"Ye are of your father the devil, and the lusts of your father ye will do. He was a murderer from the beginning and abode not in the truth because there was no truth in him"* John 8:44. Did you catch that? There is no truth in him. The truth is Jesus Christ. Scripture says, *"I am the way, the truth, and the life, no man cometh unto the Father, but by me."* John 14:6. Suppose you have never read from Genesis to Revelation. You have no right telling someone else their view of the truth of Jesus Christ to be wrong. Read it for yourself and judge. Then, read it again. See what you think. I didn't stop with that. I went to a real anointed church to see if it was really true. Suppose you are a person who has astral projections and is into witchcraft. You know what church around is stronger. You call Christians weak because they don't stop you from cursing the neighborhoods when you come to take territory. What neighborhood did they chase you away from? What church did Satan tell you he is struggling with? Why? Because I am telling you the church that you think is opposing your kingdom has something you don't. Go and see if it is really true. I love you and want you to know this truth even if you have never been told. I love you enough to tell you the truth.

## Other Witchcraft

Did you know that in Hawaii, they sacrifice men and women to their gods? Did you know that in Tibet, they sacrifice men to their gods? Did you know in the Buddhist religion, sacrifice is necessary to appease their gods? Did you know that in Hinduism, sacrifice is necessary to appease their gods? Did you know that behind closed doors, the priestesses and priests in Mormonism sacrifice to their gods? They don't just use animal blood to cleanse from sinfulness. They use human sacrifice to appease their gods. Children sacrifice in witchcraft, and adult sacrifice in religions. Yes. These things are true. Missing people are often sacrificed to Satan and demons. The Bible talks a lot about this stuff. Get in there and dig it out. Look around you and open up your eyes. I moved to a place near a big waterway. I remember reading in the Bible about how corrupt the sea merchant lands were. Do you remember the Philistines by the waterway of the Mediterranean Sea? There was a lot that went on there. When I moved to the place, I am living now. I have walked into so many businesses and traveled through city after city by the water and am appalled that there are no Christians cursing these places to the root and tearing them down. You have the right under Christ to get rid of this. The corruption is from a lack of prayer. Prayerless people. I am speaking not only to you but to myself. I am working out my salvation too. We have to understand one thing. We were put into a war when we accepted Christ. If you don't want to fight, you may not have entered the military. But you did, my sister, my brother, you did. I challenge you to pray. Pray like you never have before. Drive to these places and tear them down in the spirit if you pray in tongues. Great. Tear them down that way. Use the words that were given to you. You must know how to pray in your language too. The Lord gave you authority in Christ to pluck up, tear down, destroy, bind, and loose, didn't he?

There is another thing I saw on the Brady bunch growing up. There was this episode where they went to Hawaii, I believe. On the trip, they saw these figures. I see them in a restaurant in one city for a separate religion. Then, an hour and a half away, I see them on the street now for sale. I want to mention the place they are for sale on the street is a city I see held by witchcraft. I see in this city, there are various things the people called Christians are allowing. There are Buddhist statues for sale and held in yards to protect their homes. I see many things. There are serious strongholds in the cities by the water. Strongholds of Mosques, Buddhism, Polytheism, Animism, Liquor stores, Nightclubs, Wandering souls on the street, and Churches of Satan. In Santeria, an oricha called, Eleguá is made out of clay or earth to form a mask. They, again, are fallen angels. The people in Santeria worship them, as they believe these deities are set in place by Olodumare, their creator. The ones in Hawaii and in the United States I see are the same. They are full figures that stand about 3 or 4 feet high. They are made of wood. The Lord said in Exodus 20 and Deuteronomy 5 to not make for yourselves these things and bow down to them. These are actual beings God created, and people are making idols out of them and worshipping them. It is a sin. It is what we could go to hell for. The Lord God and Father, His Jesus, and Holy Spirit are only to be worshipped. If we worship things and beings that were created by him, we have no love for our true Creator. The Father, Son, and Holy Spirit are One God. There are no three gods here. They are One.

## Hinduism

Did you know that the Avatar is a Hindu concept? We were dumbed down by it in video games and movies of the 80s and 90s, and 2000s on up. Are they okay with God? I am not sure. I see they came from the root of Hinduism.

The Bible says, *"wherein in time past ye walked according to the course of this world, according to the prince of the power of air, the spirit that now worketh in the children of disobedience: among whom also we all had our conversation in times past in the lusts of our flesh, fulfilling the desires of the flesh and the mind; and were by nature the children of wrath, even as others"* Ephesians 2:2-3.

Did you read that? I want to ensure my eye gate and ear gate and all gates are held by the LORD. What does he want us to do? Can he use it for good with the evil that was intended? I know he uses for good the evil that was intended, what he says about this. I am not sure yet. I am concerned about it in my gates.

The Avatar is now used on screen to manifest fallen angels' qualities. The fallen angel, called Vishnu, can manifest in a person. He can manifest through ground demons in you, or he can come down and live in you for a time too. These are things the Lord allows if you are in possession of the enemy. If you have never received Jesus as your Lord and Savior, the enemy can live in your spirit and dwell there. These things are true facts. It is known to the Hindus that Avatar has moved to fall into the communities it wants entry. Thus, the Christian church. The Avatar, called Vishnu, is Satan or a fallen angel. Vishnu, Avatar, is known to be one of the three Trinity divinities for Hinduism. Vishnu is said to be very peaceful and so loving. He is known to be the one who is capable of the preservation and sustaining of the world of animals and humans. He is known to be full of righteousness. Wow! This is so awful! He is taking on characteristics of our one and only God. He is the giver of Mantras, so they say. So, if you are into Mantras, you are into Satan. Don't be deceived. This is from the devil. Vishnu, or as they call him, other names of Narayana or Hari, wanted to jump over the airwaves, and he succeeded. The Prince of the air is the ruler of the Game Networks, the Internet, Movies, and Television. If you think differently, you do not understand when the Lord tells you he is the Prince of the power of the air. If he is the Prince, then he is the ruler. Therefore, the Prince put forth the Avatar so you would follow him. He got into your mind and ears that way. Get him out of your gates. Get him out of your homes and offices and wherever you have allowed him to be. If you think I just don't give Satan the credit, you are, Kathleen. Well, you can think that. But from what I have learned and been through and have seen and read in Scripture, I think differently. Do I have it all together? Nope! I am still working out my salvation with fear and trembling. Fear and trembling. Help me and us, Lord, to follow you and clean up our lives your way. Do I hear the demons knocking, but do you like video games, still? Yes, I played them until 2011; I don't play them no more. Is there hope in that part of networking? Yes.

Creations of things that are good with God are right. Would I play again? Probably, not. Because I want God to use me to do more work, I don't have a television. I do have the phone. Yes, I see videos on it. Can the devil still get in that way? Yep. I shut lots of things off even though I buy them on Up Faith and Family. Why? Because I have walked a hard road and seen a lot of crazy things. I am a server of Jesus who reads the Bible constantly. God pours into me this way. I can make sense of the crazy things I have been through. I was in a community with other people who had walked crazy roads, and we talked twice a month, and we helped one another through prayer. I have served to help others who are vulnerable and hurting. I am part of a Kingdom people now and am operating under a great covering of Apostle, David E. Taylor.

## Secret Societies

Secret Societies say that there is a Creator. They do not say that Jesus Christ is LORD and the only way to heaven. They do not say that the Father is God who sent Jesus here to save mankind. They do not say that the Father and Jesus sent the Holy Spirit here. They do not say that there is One God who exists as three separate persons, Father, Son, and

Holy Ghost. Secret Societies operate in witchcraft. They are secret men or women societies that are into ritualistic things. These are ritualistic things like Santeria and Palo Mayombe. I have seen them throughout my life hurting people. They claim to love and want to help the people in the community. They resemble peacefulness but are inward in sorrow and trouble. They are often held by the power of money or greatness. They are known as Abakua, Rebekah's, Job's Daughters, Odd Fellows, Fraternities, Sororities, and so on. There are many others. These places harness demons in men and women who use them to perform evil deeds on earth. If you are in or have been a part of these things, you may have open doors to the enemy. If you have never closed them, the enemy has legal rights. These are communities of Satan. I am sorry if you believe differently because you have friends that you have made here. It is wrong. You probably had a check and ignored it. It is not of God.

# Chapter 15 - Drumming

During their drumming circles, they have a meal to share with each other. The Bible says, *"Let their table become a snare before them: And that which should have been for their welfare, let it become a trap"* Psalm 69:22. You will not receive the Lord Jesus; this is the problem. In this circle, you are calling on fallen angels and Satan. The Bible says, *"Thou shalt not suffer a witch to live"* Exodus 22:18. The people in these communities need to repent, or they will not live. They must turn to Jesus before it is too late. God loves you; turn to him through Christ and be saved.

Drumming circles are a way for those in the church of Satan to communicate with fallen angels to receive from them. They believe they are bringing forth Mayan energy. That was the same energy that killed children on the altars. Yes, they are bringing that energy for the gods to bring murder down and cause them to sacrifice humans to them. They play their instruments and sing to what they believe are their gods. Their events last five hours or more, and they believe they are getting healing and information from the principalities whom they call gods. The information they want to receive from their gods is how to further their medicinal and holistic community. They share what has been taught with them to others. The essential oils and the medicines of herbs and such. They believe there will be healing in this. They believe that the gods will heal them. The people believe that when they sing certain songs, the oricha or deity likes, then it will come and possess one of them. The deity will either reprimand people in the crowd or tell them good things about life.

In this event, drumming circles are using Labyrinths. I am saddened that Christian pastors and churches are using these. You are now moving out of the light. You are entertaining fallen angels (principalities). You believe in drawing closer to Jesus by doing this, but in fact, you are pushing him out of your life. This is not a path of peace. You are kicking him out of the church and letting Satan in. These Labyrinths are a trap. You are trapped now in the occult. The Labyrinth is evil. I remember when I was a kid, and the movie Labyrinth came out. I had a check in my spirit not to watch it, just like in The Never-ending Story. I didn't know about checks back then. But I ignored it and watched. It was a trap for me then, and it is a trap now. The Labyrinth that was designed for King Minos was a way for the principality to take on the characteristics of the identity of this king. With his evil ways, the principality formed as his own. Furthermore, those in the church who let Snow White, and the Wizard of Oz captivate them are entertaining devils to enter your subconscious mind. They want to access it here. Thus, they can play on your emotions and bring more evil shows into your life to gain more access. Do you want to know what Satan says to God? It is that you have allowed him in, and he has legal rights to do things until you repent, renounce, and close these doors. Your eyes, ears, mind, nose, mouth, consciousness, and subconsciousness are gateways. Go to the Scriptures and read about it. It is in there.

Labyrinths and mazes are a way for you to communicate with the earth. It is also the way that it is known for you to go to the underworld. The people who do these things are doing things associated with Satan and his fallen angels (principalities). You are coming in contact with them. Though, in the witchcraft world in their religions, it is believed that hell isn't real because they believe in all going to the spirit world. But it is known that the Labyrinth is an entry to the underworld. If it is known, the enemy is telling you the truth, and you are blinded. He is telling you that you will end up in hell... It is a known fact that there is one way in mazes (labyrinths). One way is what is told to get to the center to find balance and sacred space and to another world. Yes, you will get to another place. But the Bible tells us that there is one way. Scripture says, *"I am the way, the truth, and the life: no man cometh to the Father, but by me"* John 14:6. However, witches and wizards, and warlocks believe in one supreme God who is not accessible. They do not believe that Jesus is God. They do not believe the Holy Spirit is God. They do not believe Father is God. Christians believe in one God. This God is three persons, Father, Son, and Holy Spirit. He is one God. They agree. They don't change. Witchcraft religion believes the Supreme Creator is the person who created them, but that they can only communicate with his deities, not straight to him. These deities communicate with them along with their demons on the ground. They communicate with Satan, who is a deity to them. They believe Jesus is their spirit guide and that he is a medium.

The labyrinth stones in these labyrinth circles are considered sacred by these people. They treat them as having the ability to give readings. You are getting readings from them like tarot cards. The principality now has the ability to affect your future and generations. It is believed that you are contacting a god and a goddess. The principalities here are referred to as him or her. Therefore, there are two of them.

Drumming circles under the witchcraft circles use the Santerían ritual of dancing, singing, and drumming that an oricha will possess someone. They are using divination to understand the words that the oricha is saying to them. The people will be told to get the oricha (fallen angel) a cigar and liquor. You may have seen people walking around Louisiana practicing voodoo with a cigar in their mouth. Voodoo is big in Santeria too. Also, get out of singing bowl meditation too. It is witchcraft.

# Sports Bars and Psychics

**This is a gathering place people eat and watch sports and drink. You might be a Christian that goes to this place. Little do you know that this bar is haunted by witches and wizards and those of the dark side that know how to take you down. They will enter your family through any member of your family who goes here to take down your family; this includes brothers, sisters, etc. They are after you. Once you have your cards read, you now have a demon that will follow you home and be upon, in, and through you.**

You may gather at a sports bar for a game and beer, but you truly are being sucked into walking after the ways of the world. You might be a Christian that goes to this place. Little do you know that bars are haunted by witches and wizards and those of the dark side that know how to take you down. They will enter your family through any member of your family who goes here to take down your family; this includes brothers, sisters, etc. They are after you. The enemy is out for the destruction of a family.

Once you have your cards read, you now have demons that follow you home and are upon, in, and through you. A psychic is a person who is skilled at hearing from demons. They believe they hear from good and bad spirits. The thing is, they hear from familiar spirits. The familiar spirits that came in with you, who's followed you around all your life and know about you, communicate with the demon inside of them to tell you about your past. They will tell you what you are doing now too. Then, they will tell you about the future. How? They will tell you what their ideas are. That is, the demon speaking through the person to you or telling the person what to say to you will tell you what they want to see for your life. The cards are manipulated to bring destruction to you and your spouse and family. They might be doing it through riches or through something else you read in the cards. Then, what happens? You have now given legal rights over for the demons to make this happen. You are now in their hands for these things to happen. You will see them happen, and you are supposed to go back to the medium when they do. Then, you will have to pay a lot of money to do something called a ritual to get rid of the bad things that will come. The rituals put you into contracts with principalities. These principalities now have you by your britches through contracts. I have learned through John Ramirez, mentoring me in these things. John has shared that there are Satanic Courts and Demonic Courts in the heavens. You may have your name on these courts. You have legal papers and scrolls up there all about you and your life. If you want this to stop, you must learn spiritual warfare and satanic warfare. It is a battle, and if you're not fighting it through Jesus Christ and by the power of his Holy Spirit, you are not winning. You are walking defeated. You need the Son to have the Father and the Son to have the Holy Ghost.

## Demonic Tongues

Did you know that in the church of Satan, the congregants learn demonic tongues? These tongues can be given at home or in the church. They are to mimic the tongue given by the Holy Spirit. Satan and demons have manipulated what was done during Pentecost with the 120 people in the upper room to fool people. The people who receive the demonic tongue could believe they are Christian and receiving the Holy

Spirit tongues. They could also believe that they are receiving a language from the spirit world. Spirits manipulate the demonic tongues. They seek to mimic the real thing. They may start you off with one word repeated. Then, if you are a Christian and have broken free and received the prayer langue through the baptism of the Holy Spirit, you may still need deliverance from this. In this case, the spirit will manipulate and deceive you and try to copy the Holy Spirit's words to fool you more.

*"And when the day of Pentecost was fully come, they were all with one accord in one place. And suddenly there came a sound from heaven as of a rushing mighty wind, and it filled all the house where they were sitting. And there appeared unto them cloven tongues like of fire, and it sat upon each of them. And they were all filled with the Holy Ghost, and began to speak with other tongues, as the Spirit gave them utterance. And there were dwelling at Jerusalem Jews, devout men, out of every nation under heaven. Now when this was noised abroad, the multitude came together, and were confounded, because that every man heard them speak in his own language. And they were amazed and marvelled, saying one to another, Behold, are not all these which speak Galilaeans? And how hear we every man in our own tongue, wherein we were born? Parthians, and Medes,*

*and Elamites, and the dwellers in Mesopotamia, and in Judea, and Capadocia, in Pontus, and Asia, Phrygia, and Pamphylia, in Egypt, and in parts of Libya and Cyrene and strangers of Rome, Jews and proselytes, Cretes and Arabians, we do hear them speak in our tongues the wonderful works of God."* Acts 2:1-11

Can you imagine? The people of God, Jews, who wrote by the inspiration of the Holy Spirit, discuss in Scripture that there were many people from all over who converted to Judaism. The people who lived in Iran, Iraq, Judea (southern Israel), Turkey, Libya, Rome, Saudia Arabia, and so on. God touches men's hearts to speak a language from heaven to God. The people in other languages can hear and understand that heavenly language. The one given the language has no clue what they are speaking unless you get the interpretation.

# Chapter 16 - Strong Men

You have Allah (principality) worship in this town. This has brought death and suicide spirits. Note the moon on top. He is the moon god.

The god called Allah is an extremely dangerous god. He will fight if you try to bring him down in your communities. The demons on the ground will go crazy. But you have to understand you are not taking down the demons on the ground. You are dealing with a strong man. He is a principality; in this case, he is above the ground demons. I am fighting him now. He is strong. He is strong because there are so many of his people praying to him in this area. There are mosques everywhere. There are many small mosques all around. This principality doesn't want to lose ground here. The people were planted here. They were brought over from the Middle East to live here. The Bible says, "*And the angel of the LORD said unto her (Hagar), Return to your mistress (Sarai), and submit thyself under her hands. And the angel of the LORD said unto her, I will multiply thy seed exceedingly, it shall not be numbered for multitude. And the angel of the LORD said unto her, behold, thou art with child, and shalt bear a son, and shalt call his name Ishmael because the LORD hath heard thy affliction. And he will be a wild man, his hand will be against every man, and every man's hand against him, and he shall dwell in the presence of all his brethren." Genesis 16:9-12.*

The Muslim people are known to be wild. They are wild indeed and numerous. The Lord blessed them; they are many. God blesses people to have children. This is a characteristic blessing of the Lord to have a family. Family is good. The Muslim people believe they are true believers. They believe that Christians worship three gods. We worship One God existent in three persons. Muslims are confused about Jesus being called the Son of God. They believe we think that God had sex with Mary to produce Jesus. This is weird. No, we believe he is incarnate and born by the working of the Holy Spirit, putting him in Mary by God's own power, not through Joseph. I believe Muslims can accept this. They believe Jesus was a prophet. They believe that Jesus will return in the Second Coming. The Muslims (Shia and Sunni) both believe that an Imam Mahdi will be a living person called Muhammad. They believe that very soon, this Mahdi will appear and make the Muslims that are of Shia, and Sunni be together again. They have different beliefs. This Mahdi is believed to be alive at the coming of Jesus. They believe Jesus will set things right here on earth.

Muhammad was thought to have heard from who he believed to be Gabriel, the Arch Angel, to write the Quran. What Muhammad heard was an angel appearing as an angel of light. I understand this well. You can get confused thinking you hear from heaven and write what appears as great words of wisdom from God. They are words that seem right. They are mixed with Jewish and Christian truths. They have a way of making it seem right, like Satan, tempting Jesus with the Word of God. They have truths in them, but it is to twist it to be for Satan and his kingdom to bring more people to hell with him. The Bible says, *"And God said unto Abraham, as for Sarai, thy wife, thou shalt not call her name Sarai, but Sarah shall her name be. And I will bless her and give thee a son also of her; yea, I will bless her, and she shall be a mother of nations; kings of people shall be of her. Then Abraham fell upon his face, and laughed, and said in his heart, shall a child be born unto him that is a hundred years old? And shall Sarah, that is ninety years old, bear? And Abraham said unto God, O that Ishmael might live before thee! And God said, Sarah, thy wife shall bear thee a son; indeed, and thou shalt call his name Isaac: and I will establish my covenant, and with his seed after him. And as for Ishmael, I have heard thee: Behold, I have blessed him, and will make him fruitful, and will multiply him exceedingly; twelve princes shall he beget, and I will make him a great nation. But my covenant will I establish with Isaac, which Sarah shall bear unto thee at this set time in the next year. And God went up from Abraham"* Genesis 17:15-22.

The covenant was established with Sarah, and the Jewish nation was born through Abraham, Isaac, and Jacob. Now, Muslims are supposed to hold to reading only the books of Moses, Psalms, and the Gospels. This is it from the Bible. They believe that Jesus is the Word of God. They do not understand that the Bible is the written Word of God, all about Jesus, and he communicates to us through it. They hold that other books were lost, like Enoch and such. They believe that God put forth to read only Genesis, Exodus, Leviticus, Numbers, Deuteronomy, Psalms, and Matthew through John in the Bible and the Quran. You may have heard Muslims say to you we have altered the books of the Bible. This, perhaps, is why they don't study them well. The Quran has translations, too, many translations. I explain just like the words are used differently by generations; the translations are written for new generations to understand them. They write their Quran this way too. The Bible is not altered; it has the same God working the same way with his words. In some translations, you will find that words should not have been shortened. In King James Version, you find more words to get a better understanding than in other translations. They will read the Quran because they believe that it has never been altered. This is what they believe about Christians and our Bible today: "By Allah, we did certainly send messengers to nations before you, but Satan made their deeds attractive to them. And he is the disbelievers' ally today as well, and they will have a painful punishment. We have sent down the Book (Quran) that you may explain to them the truth concerning what they are disputing and that the Book may serve as a guidance and mercy for those who believe in it" (Quran 16:63-64). Therefore, they believe that we are mistaken, and that the Quran holds value over the Scriptures in the Bible. You may want to ask them about doing good works to get to heaven. They believe that their good works will help them get to heaven. This is a way for you to explain what Jesus did for us. He did what we couldn't do. If a man believes in Justice when we are hurt on this earth. Then, we believe that God is a just God and will need to punish sin. If we all admit that we do commit sins, then we need a just God to punish sin. We cannot do enough good works to receive mercy from God. God had to punish sin in a sinless man, and Jesus (Yeshua) was the only person who did what we couldn't do. The Muslims are not sure that Allah will forgive them. They believe in purgatory. They believe that Muhammad prays for them and that even in purgatory, Muhammad's prayers could free them. They believe that suicidal killings get them into heaven. They are not sure of many things, and they do fear greatly on this earth. Explain to them that Jesus did what we couldn't do. Explain what he did for you. They hold Jesus extremely high in regard. There is a fact that they believe if they betray Allah and listen to our teachings to pursue another God, like our One and only God, they cannot ever be forgiven. So, please understand they are truly in fear of accepting our teachings. They are to lead us to their god, Allah. This is their mission. They want us to convert that we might have life.

# Mammon

**I want you to see that cat. It is a stronghold of a god.**

The strongman Mammon. This is a strongman, just like Buddha is a strongman. The cat symbolizes a charm. Charms are witchcraft. I see them in the church and out of the church. I mentioned before about a vagabond strongman, a principality. Money is a strongman too. If you are poor, you might want to be rich. You might be wrapped in it in your mind and will. You may play the lottery. I can still tell you the numbers my parents played, and that was from before 1992. I had them memorized because we played the lottery at least twice a week. The leadings of Mammon will make you constantly play the lottery to get rich. This is not God's way. He has a way, and that is to trust him in your finances. Your finances are to be put in his hands. I have much testimony with this. I remember in 1996; I believed I was going to become a member of the First Baptist Church. I had meetings with different people in the church. One meeting was with the person who did the finances in the church. She told me that to be a member, I needed to give 10 percent of my income to God. I had not had a hard time until I came to this meeting. That seemed impossible. I barely paid the bills. The word was planted, though. I kept learning about this 10 percent until 2012. It took me that many years to submit my finances to God. A lot of people get hung up here. I have been provided for in so many ways by submitting to God's way. I believe this because I truly tested God here. He was right. If you choose to follow God this way, expect people to not believe you inside the church and outside of it. I hear so many people who do not get this concept. They will tell me the pastors are wrong. God is not wrong. If we are under his leadership in this area, we will get out of debt too. We have to do work on our part too. He doesn't do everything. But he can do much with our little obedience. He said to be faithful in the small things (money).

Back to the charms, I know that this spans the church. You may see people wearing necklaces for luck. These charms can be statements too. I see in the essential oil industry people operating in witchcraft here. That picture above is witchcraft. If you put that up, you are putting up Mammon's contract you made with him in your finances. A contract is made when you speak aloud affirmations to get money and attract people to you to grow your business too. Words have the power to kill and bring to life. The demons hear you when you speak things over you for people and money to come to you when you use your essential oils. They are now in your life to bring these things to your life. You get a spirit, not the living God. Get out of wearing and putting up charms for Mammon. A similar factor is in Hollywood and the Music Industry. You make an agreement with Mammon to give you fortune and success.

# Chapter 17 – Halloween

He is charming a snake. This is their New Year.

Many churches and cities are controlled by witchcraft because they allow Halloween to be celebrated. You may think I am ridiculous. You give candy to the kids in the community as a Christian. I understand that it is possible that some wrap Scriptures around the candy and give it to the Trick or Treaters that come to your door. This is still participating. Do I think eating wrapped candy with a Halloween wrapper is wrong? No. I think celebrating Halloween is what is wrong. I have been told by Christians that I am the one with the problem. I have been told that there is nothing wrong with celebrating Halloween if you are a Christian and that this is loving the kids in the community. I have been in church and celebrated Halloween with kids for a long time. The church is involved in the community of Trunk or Treat or Fall Festival. It is still celebrating Halloween; you are still participating. Satan still has legal rights over you in the courts of Heaven. You are deceived; you celebrate Satan. Did you know that you have demons that are allowed now in your church to afflict the people because you are allowing this to continue? Did you know you have them in your home, and they are oppressing you by allowing the worship of Satan to continue in your household? You are not free because you have them controlling you in this area of your life. I am bothered about this. I see even in the church rummage sales; there are people in the church bringing all their witches and wizard things from Halloween to be sold. What? The church allows it. Why? You celebrate Halloween. Halloween is Satan's Birthday. The Samhain is the witches' New Year. They celebrate both. This month is the most onslaught against Christians. The other month is December.

Satan's purpose with you celebrating Halloween is ultimately to kill you. He will start by stealing from you through your lack of understanding. Then, he will destroy you with his witches and wizards. Then, he could kill you. You must repent of celebrating this and renounce the demons you have given access to. You may not like this picture in a Christian book. I get it. I don't like seeing children looking at it at the grocery store. Especially the Halloween movie picture on the Redbox. It is a disfigured spirit. I put the witch one above here to teach you the truth. This is what angels who fell look like; they are not good-looking. Hell is real. Their faces are disfigured. Satan uses real images. Then, the demons use fear tactics to send you to be a paralyzed woman or man. A paralyzed Christian is not an active Christian.

"Halloween and November 1st are when the strongest attacks come out of the enemy's camps. Halloween because it's the devil's holiday, and November 1st because it's called All Saint's Day, but the reality is that it's all Demon's Day. While they make you think you're celebrating dead relatives, preparing meals and food, and paying your respects at the cemeteries, the reality is that you're doing it all to demons. For twenty-five years, those were my practices. Regarding Halloween, I believe the church should rise up and do night vigils to destroy the witchcraft and diabolical rituals that go on throughout the night. These rituals are aimed toward the church to weaken us in the Spirit. So, we need to stop celebrating "Harvest" and dressing up in costumes as biblical characters that are just trying to Christianize Halloween by putting Jesus' name on it, which is not even biblical. Instead, we must be armed and fighting spiritually for our neighborhoods and those who don't know Jesus."[2]

In 2011 or 2012, I sat across from a pastor at work. We talked all day. He explained to me that he was supposed to be a Priest. He was Catholic. But one day, a Father watched him and said to him that he looked at women too much to be a priest. So, he left the Catholic church. He explained to me that Halloween was wicked and the true holiday, All Saints Day, was not being celebrated right. But Catholics celebrate dead people. They pray to saints and angels. They have feasts for dead relatives. How do you know that person is even in heaven? Anyhow, in time I went to Saint Michaels and even Saint Mary's. I learned more about witchcraft ways. You buy candles to pray to Saints as a Catholic and in Santeria... It is witchcraft. Christian witchcraft.

The reason it is sacred to the witches and warlocks is they bring spirits offerings and talk to dead relatives. It is a holiday called Samhain. The candy is supposed to be given to kids in honor of their ancestors. The ancestors are returning as children, and these same children are the ancestors through reincarnation. So, the church of Satan in spiritualism says they don't believe in reincarnation, but they mix religious beliefs and allow it in. The candles and lightened jack-o-lanterns are in honor of the dead relatives. They do these things as a ritual. The candy and jack-o-lanterns are rituals to bring spirits in to give them better health, life, and community and to make things new again for them. This is not biblical. Celebrating this way is honoring Satan. This is the true meaning of what communities are doing, and they may not even have a clue. This is a contract in heaven with an angel. You need to understand this is to be broken in the spirit realm off you and your family. It is continuing the ritual and putting generational curses on our kids. The witches are unhappy if you promote not celebrating this holiday. It is their most sacred holiday of the year. They especially want to go to school and to the news to promote this holiday. This is what the witchcraft church teaches. The witches say that they are happy that more people support Halloween than try to go against it. This is their true wish. That all people would come to their understanding of how sacred this time is in the year.

# Chapter 18 -Christmas Time in Demon Church

This is a church of Satan. It is their Christmas celebration. They celebrate the fact that they have Christians in their church. Buddhists and others in their church. They indoctrinate them on how to connect to the world of the unseen. The world of demon possession and astral projection.

The Metaphysical Church is Satan's Church. Please read what they are doing. At Christmas is their onslaught against Christians.

"In the first week of December, the witches and warlocks are preparing themselves to usher out principalities and powers to another region and bring in new ones. Sometimes you see a drastic change in the neighborhood or region, with a dramatic shift from one demonic situation to another. They keep things fresh this way and keep things on the move, so they can stay one step ahead of the church. The kingdom of darkness always wants to be one step ahead of the church because it wants to be in control. As an ex-devil worshipper, I attended these meetings. *"And from the time of John the Baptist began preaching until now, the Kingdom of Heaven has been forcefully advancing, and violent people are attacking it" (Matt. 11:12 NLT).* It goes without saying that all believers should pray at all times, but for a targeted approach, I recommend the following. In early December, instead of going to the mall and thinking about buying gifts, we should be armed and ready spiritually to destroy the works of the devil. We should be armed and ready through both corporate prayer and in the personal prayer closet to destroy the enemy's plans *"so that no advantage would be taken of us by Satan, for we are not ignorant of his schemes (2 Cor. 2:11 NASB)."*[2]

Why would a church of Satan be celebrating Jesus, anyway? They believe Jesus is the chief helper. He is the guide in the life of a medium. They see through divination Jesus as an image guiding them. Jesus is believed while he was on earth to have been a medium. Therefore, as a psychic, Jesus is honored. He is honored as the medium guiding them in the spirit world. The spirit world is a very sacred place for the people in the church of Satan. The church of Satan compromises many religions. They use the texts from various religions and hold them as of much value. The world they know is very much held by demonic powers. They see them and are held by them.

# Atheism, Polytheism, and Pantheism

**The picture was taken from the Church of Satan, Metaphysical.**

**Buddha in a position of prayer.**

Buddha was a man. He is the teacher that they revere. However, if you are using him as a teacher, you are really worshipping him as a god. The funny thing is that they say it could be atheistic in the sense that he is not a god. However, you, in reality, by putting him up in your homes and churches, are worshipping this god. It is a god. This god looks to me as a principality. This principality has stretched countries. The principality takes on identities. See, where the principality had a name in heaven, that angel of darkness was kicked out of heaven and now takes on another identity. Where the name of Jezebel was strong for wickedness, there is one Principality that has taken on that name. There are principalities that control astrology in the Zodiac too. The Zodiac (Mazzaroth) is not wicked. The Mazzaroth (Zodiac) God created with constellations. We see great light on earth because of the stars. But Satan wanted to take what God created and use it for wickedness. Job talked about it in the Bible. The Christian church may not have an understanding of stars, so it could be thought of as Satan. This is wrong thinking.

If you are receiving learning from Buddha, you are worshipping something you venerate and taking on his characteristics. This is an angelic force that took on the identity of Buddha. People believe in Nirvana and Karma. If you sing Nirvana, you are entertaining this god in your ears, heart, mouth, and mind. He has legal rights on you in the courts of Demons and also if it goes to the court of Satan. From there, Satan can go to the Court of God. You have given your rights as a Christian over to this angelic entity. You must understand you are not just walking this earth as a person who is to pick up everything on television and the radio into your mind and voice. You give Satan legal rights when you do this stuff. If you have allowed him to entertain you and now are singing these things and telling others about them, this is in the realm of a demonic curse.

Nirvana is not a state without suffering, desire, self, and karma. You are not going into rebirth and freed to Nirvana. This is false teaching from a false god. You are, in fact, worshipping a false god. Atheistic belief in no god is worshipping demons. Polytheistic gods are the multiple gods' religion. There are multiple gods: one Satan, principalities, and demons under them.

Pantheistic belief is when we hear people on television say I will send my voice into the universe, and someone will hear it. This religion tolerates all gods. Did you know in China, Taoism is a form of worship for many people? They worship fallen beings. They believe the universe is God. But in fact, words have power, and when you open yourself to speaking into the universe as God, you open yourself up to demons having great access to determine your life. Demons will control your life, not you. The principality will give demons orders to take you down.

**The Church of Satan celebrates this. They make origami and charm bracelets. This is why you need to get an inventory of your home.**

Get charm bracelets and things of charms out of your home. Not all charm bracelets are bad. But if you do not understand where it came from and of what sort it is, it could easily have things attached to it. If you have these things in your home, you have given the enemy access to your home. You need to ensure you do not celebrate the things of Satan.

# Winter Solstice and Yule Tide

This is not a Christian event. Christians refer to Yule Tide and bring songs about it. It is of the church of Satan. Wake up. It is to bring a negative circle around the church of Jesus, the Christian church. Though, at the church of Satan, it is to bring good to them in the upcoming calendar year. The people of Satan believe it will bring good things and take away negative things throughout the past year. The Yule Tide celebration should never be in the true church of Jesus Christ. It is a way for the witches and wizards of Satan to praise and celebrate the gods and goddesses. This is who these people are thanking at this celebration ritual. Christians need to become aware and stop using this in the church. This is an ancient Celtic and German worship of Satan and demons. The Satanic circle casts a negative wheel around

Christians, especially those who give way to celebrating in the song Yuletide.

## Satanic Celebration

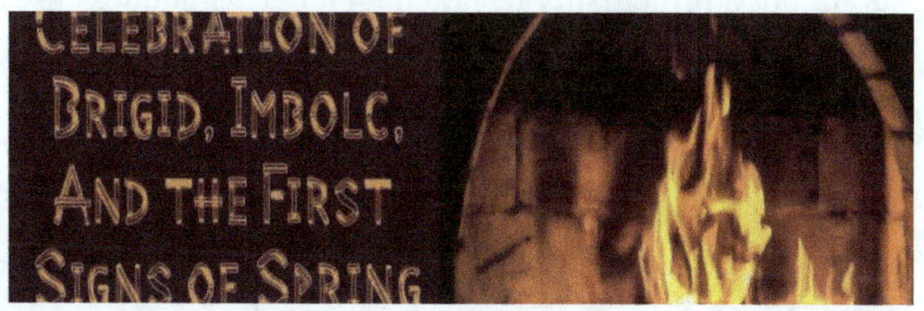


The church of Satan celebrates at the end of January, or the beginning of February Satanic ritual called, Imbolic. They call on Brigid or Bridget, a goddess of the home. They believe Imbolic Brigid will help the spring be fruitful. They are inviting spirits to come to their home and help them in the world and in the upcoming spring. This is to help them fight more in the realm of territory in the neighborhoods. They want a blessed house for them and to do evil in the world for the Christians.

The sad thing is that Christians even celebrate this in the form of a Mass called St. Bridget. This is evil. This is a goddess that is a principality. She is a god of fertility. She is a god of poetry, crafts, and prophecy. This is very evil. If you invoke this god in your life, you will start hearing voices and start down a journey of thinking you have psychic abilities. The Celtics worshipped this god. The Wiccans and pagans celebrate this goddess. It is between Yuletide and Ostara (spring equinox). Bridget is called a bride. The Bride is the church, not a principality or fallen angel. This goddess uses the element of fire. This is another reason the Christian church needs to exercise warfare authority on fire, water, earth, and wind. Yes. There are times when the Church of Satan is known to use these elements as a weapon against the church. Suppose you want to know what to do during this celebration of Imbolic. You need to exercise your authority over fire because the church of Satan is calling on this principality to exercise it over you. The water is a place of water and marine spirits. I deal with them in the month, understanding what is going on in the heavens with the moon.

You need to exercise your authority that this principality will bring no healing for his people. This is what they believe the goddess, Brigit gives them abilities to do smith work and poetry. They believe that they get these things from this goddess. They believe they can contact this goddess through divination and get more divination powers from it. They can succeed. Christian, please understand what happened with Nebuchadnezzar.

*"Appoint a way, that the sword may come to Rabbah of the Ammonites, and to Judah in Jerusalem the defenced. For the king of Babylon stood at the parting of the way, at the head of the two ways, to use divination; he made his arrows bright, he consulted with images, he looked in the liver. At his right hand was the divination for Jerusalem, to appoint captains, to open the mouth in the slaughter, to lift up the voice with shouting, to appoint battering rams against the gates, to cast mount, and to build fort. And it shall be unto them as a false divination in their sight, to them that have sworn oaths; but he will call to remembrance the iniquity, that they may be taken"* Ezekiel 21:20-23

This was a way the kingdom of darkness was able to get into Judah. The people were unaware of the crossing of the ritual of the road that was done with blood. This was able to lock them down in the spirit and the physical. If the people knew about warfare better in the church today, they would know this is how they are still locked down. This is why you see little moving in the church and neighborhoods and lives of Christians. If you want to counter, get to your corners, and unlock yourself and your neighborhood and church. Divination always has to do with seeing images. If you see images and think, you see visions from God. You may be seeing a tool of the enemy called prophetic divination images. You must ensure it is the real God giving you a vision. False visions are different.

## Summer Solstice

**Christian, this is a time to be fighting. Not sleeping.**

The church of Satan is celebrating Lilith. This is a ritualistic time too. They are celebrating the fertility of evil. It may be for some to see a great amount of evil like sex, drugs, and rock and roll. The church of Satan will be doing cleansing too to get rid of things to be able to be filled with the deities' desire to live out in their lives what he or she desires.

# Chapter 19 - Children Deceived in Our Generations

I am closing the book by talking about my own experience in the public school system. I want to show you what is in the world too. Here in my life is a big evil going on that was in times past and is now covered up under another term to fool our generations. When I say our generations, I am talking about the terms Baby Boomers, Generation X, Y, Z, A, and so forth. This is how Satan fools us. He changes the terms to fool you. I have talked about it in this book already. But now I want to close by showing you what is done.

In past decades, this was a way for Satan to deceive the generations.

In past decades, the way Satan deceived the masses and children was through haunted funeral homes and haunted houses. He uses these things to get you into the Principality Jezebel. Jezebel in the heavens is a principality that puts fear in people. John Ramirez has twenty-one steps of her dismantling a person in their life and stealing their anointing if they are a Christian. I had this happen to me. It is very real. Fear is one of the steps Jezebel, the Principality, uses to dismantle you in your life. If Jezebel can dismantle you here. You will not be effective in living out the life God intended for you. You may be immobilized from finishing your mission on earth; in Elijah's case, he fasted to get this off of him. This way, God could use him to finish his mission on earth. The person that is a Christian has something that God has intended them for on this earth. Elijah's fasting was able to break this off of him to complete his assignment.

The movie Escape Room is to bring a spirit into your life. There is a spirit called fear. It is a real spirit operating under Satan. It is real. If you think fear is normal for every person. You are wrong. Fear is a spirit. I understand this well. It is a spirit sent to you from Satan's kingdom. Anytime you have a fear come over you, it is a demonic force working in the unseen realm or Satan himself. You cannot see the unseen. I have only seen it at times. I have seen it, and it is real. But I want you to understand that Escape Rooms are going up all over the United States. They are everywhere in Michigan now. I want you to know that I have talked to someone working at one of them. The person was excited to work there. You know when you open yourself up to this stuff. You are under the control of Satan and his kingdom. You cannot have birthday parties there and go into the different rooms to be given clues to get out of the rooms and not understand that it is Satan. The mystery is entering the realm of your mind and subconsciousness, which the enemy wants to access. It is still operating in the realm of the fear devils. If you are unaware of this stuff, please be advised it is a deception, and you are being deceived. There are spirits of sleeping, slumbering, fear, and deception. I want you to understand you need Jesus, and you need to renounce these things. Renounce these places, these movies, these fear, tormenting devils. You have a stronghold demon now in your life. Get out of watching movies like The Forever Purge and Don't Breathe. The Principality cannot bring into the physical without people allowing it to come into the physical. You and I, as human beings, allow them to do this through our minds. We allow them into our ears, eyes, and minds, and there they come out of our mouths into the realm of the physical.

*"Her adversaries are the chief, her enemies prosper; for the LORD hath afflicted her for the multitude of her transgressions: her children are gone into captivity before the enemy."* Lamentations 1:5

This was a serious thing that happened to Judah. Nebuchadnezzar took Judah's children into captivity. I am in a day where Russia attacked Ukraine in February 2014 and again in February 2022. Now, their children are being taken captive by Russia. It is a tear-filled time. I cry a lot. I am so saddened by this. I tear, cry, and pray. I don't want this. This is awful. I don't want to see Ukraine in such despair. Their people are leaving for Poland and Israel in terror for their lives. At the same time, the people in Ukraine are constantly being killed and going into captivity. What does this have to do with our own children here in America? The enemy is taking America captive in their minds and working on getting a place to defeat the people in the country. This way, he tears us down to sin. Could another country come and bomb us and declare war? What happened to Judah first? The people went away from God. What we do now matters. We have to love them and care, help, pray, and repent. I am saying I cry and love Ukraine. I don't want her in captivity and in war. This is a time to pray. Ukraine has a lot of Jewish people. If we don't care for the Jews, why would God care for us? If you don't understand this and believe in replacement theology like some in the church (many), you do not understand the Bible. You don't understand that Jesus was Jewish and that we owe what we have to the Jews. They shared with us the foundational understanding of the foundation (God Jesus). I just don't want America to go down through the sins of society and through God's judgment.


# Schools

I have taught in the schools for years. What I have seen is negative. Though the kids are there to learn math, reading and English, and other subjects, they have taught them every day using witchcraft. If you don't teach that way, I commend you. But in every school I have taught, which is fifteen or more, there is witchcraft teaching in subjects. First of all, the kids, as early as kindergarten through twelfth grade, are taught witchcraft. While the kindergarteners and through second grade might only see it on occasion. The third graders may be starting this every day. But the fifth graders are using it every day. When I taught, I found ways to get them out. I was instructed to teach it, but I found creative ways to not. I told them no. I didn't get to that lesson that day and left a note that we were not able to. One day, while I was sitting in the lunchroom, a person from the office came down and talked to me. The student told their main teacher that I would not let them read the Harry Potter book. The teacher told the office, and the office came down. I was told that the students at that school could read them and there was nothing wrong with them. I have had students tell me they were pagans. One high schooler told me about seeing things moving across the room as though someone was carrying them and no one she could see carrying them. I have come into the school to have a student trying to commit suicide in the locker room while I was teaching and stopped it. I came into the school with a bomb thought to be in the building, and it was stopped. Look, the spiritual is real. There are real enemies, and if you think witchcraft books are okay for students. You are introducing them to demons.

Every day witchcraft is in the math class. Every day your kids have to play witchcraft to do their math. They use software called, Prodigy and Cool Math that uses witchcraft to teach math. The games are to cast spells in the video game to do the math. From elementary through high school, students have to play these games in math class. In the learning disabilities classrooms, the kids are constantly on the computer during the day playing games. The games are witchcraft games. Computers are instructing the kids. If you think teachers are in front of the boards talking, it's not done. Sure, there are exceptions. I see exceptions. But the computer is an extensive portion of the schoolers' day. The computer is what is teaching them. The student has an assignment. The student is doing the assignment the teacher put together, but what happens in their free time? They play games and listen to bad music on their headphones. It is allowed. The music has profane words. I caught one student looking at pornography on their phone, and I got yelled at by the principal for raising my voice in the classroom at the student. The student cursed me out when I tried to stop it.

They use the Internet to answer questions. Then, they have free time to play games. Games are the enemy's tool to steal their minds. The teachers need to wise up and change their classrooms. In Middle School, the kids are told to read their books thirty minutes before the first hour. Often, the books they have are witchcraft books.

The little ones who are still learning to read have an iPad. The iPad is full of ideas from the world that are not about kid-like things like magic games and scary books. I like the animal books on there. I guide them to them. I teach from the front of the classroom. They start learning this way.

They start learning when they use actual paper and pencils, and crayons too. Teachers in higher grades, too, do this. Teach them from the front and have them all participate.

Did you know in high school, I am asked to show movies and have them read books? As a sub, I have had teachers leaving me movies full of sex (actual sex) and lots of cursing. What? I don't want to listen and see this. Nor do I want to be responsible before a parent and God to show this to the students. On one occasion, the teacher told the Spanish class they would have four movies to choose from. I was appalled at all four. Real live sex, profane language. I stopped them; I knew some Spanish. We did Spanish that day. If the students had papers to turn in for a movie we were supposed to watch in English class, and I stopped it, I told them to let their teacher know why I stopped it. I leave teachers' notes.

## Video Games

I played video games like Pac-man, Frogger, and Crash Bandicoot. I played lots of others. I stopped them around 2010 on the game systems. I was able to visit the Psychic in Animal Crossing. Satan is the god of the air. He gets into your mind this way by playing video games. I am so sorry to my daughter for allowing so many things into the home. I bought games for my husband and her, like Grand Theft Auto. I was responsible for teaching right, and I failed. These games introduce sex and pornography, and other things. The games have advanced since then into greater evils. The game industry is a substantial portion of the reason people don't pursue things of God. There is such a spirit of slumber, addiction, and laziness attached to playing video games.

# Sources

1.      Grover S, Mehra A Dua D. Unusual cases of succubus: A cultural phenomenon manifesting as part of psychopathology. Ind Psychiatry J 2018; 27:147-150.

2.      Ramirez, John. Unmasking the Devil, Strategies to Defeat Eternity's Greatest Enemy. Destiny Image Publishers, Inc., Shippensburg, PA, 2015.

3.      Selman, Apostle Joshua (2020). The Secret God Told Me About the Sun, the Moon & The Stars [Video]. YouTube. joshua selman about the sun, moon - YouTube

4.      Taylor, David E. Miracles in America. Week 17: Jesus Descent into Hell After His Crucifixion. Ancient Writings.                              YouTube. https://youtube.com/playlist?list=PLRSrB7Wv7_nbigwYt0 eAiYQ2Wss9gIcQS&si=5zkqbY7Ms0mclKMk

All Scripture was taken from the Authorized King James Version.

Additional Text was taken from the Book of Enoch and Jasher.

# About The Author

Kathleen Spooner has worked in ministry for a while. She loves helping others be lifted up out of the miry clay. She desires to help those that may have lost their voice in life out of the situations that have enslaved them.  Kathleen has worked with troubled women ministering in word and prayer at a Rescue Mission.

She was a member of the John Ramirez Inner Circle. The Inner Circle works to help those that want the freedom in life that God designed them to live in. The group is focused on helping those who are called into the world of deliverance ministry and spiritual warfare intercessory.

She went to Liberty University and graduated in 2015 with a MA in Christian Ministry. She is ordained as a minister. The biggest accomplishment in her life is being a mother of one daughter. She has used her shame in life as a stepping stone. She is extremely thankful to Apostle Taylor for mentoring her in life. Currently, she is in the Downriver area of Detroit.